汉英对照

·

英汉注解

赵彦春国学经典英译系列

赵彦春 译·注

英韵三字经（插图本）

Three Word Primer in English Rhyme

With Illustrations

高等教育出版社·北京

出版前言

三字经，大多数学者认为约成书于南宋时代，是当时儒者王应麟为了更好地教育本族子弟读书而编写的、融会了经史子集的三字歌诀。全书涵盖知识广泛，包括教育、伦理、道德、天文、历史、地理等方面，渗透。以儒家仁、义、诚、敬、孝等思想，格式上三字一句朗朗上口，具有通俗、顺口、易记等特点，与百家姓、千字文并称为中国传统蒙学三大读物，合称『三百千』，是中国文化的入门书。

自出版以来，三字经即已通过多种文字广泛传播至中国以外的其他国家。早期传教士向异国介绍中国文化的首选典籍便是三字经。

据记载，世界上最早的三字经翻译本是成书于16世纪的拉丁文译本。此后，沙俄、韩、日等国也相继出现各种译本及仿制本。普希金甚至高度称赞其为『三字圣经』。

自南宋以来，已有多位传教士、汉学家将三字经译为英文，迄今已有十几个英文版本的三字经存世。赵彦春所译英韵三字经兼顾音、形、义三美标准，首创『三词格』，以丰厚的学术功底演绎出最美英韵三字经，独树一帜。

由于对中国博大精深的文化的理解及分属于印欧语系及汉藏语系的英汉两种语言的限制，此前的译本要么语义解释不够圆通，要么史实错误，即便前两者无可挑剔，在音形义三者的兼顾上也做得十分不够。

英韵三字经经作者多年的潜心琢磨，创造了一种以三个英

语单词对应汉语的三个字来译，并以整齐的『aabb』韵式，使译文更逼近三字经原文的语体与风格，从而将国学经典的外译推进到一个空前的高度。

全书按照内容大体分为教、知、学、史、勤五个部分，具有独特创意的绘画及图书设计充满禅机与韵味，与译文的创新及灵动浑然一体，赋予中华传统经典新的气质与内涵。同时，全书三字经文配以地道的汉语及英语诵读，轻松扫描二维码便可一键获取。

为了深入了解该书翻译的精髓，我们还配套出版了三字经英译课堂一书，具体展现翻译过程、心路历程及译文精妙所在，考察、细解与平行译本翟理斯的散体译文与王宝童韵体译文在表征方式上的差异，总结各自在经典翻译上的成败得失，并以此透视翻译的本质、翻译的原理、翻译的技巧以及翻译的过程中所涉及的种种因素、成败得失可能给予读者的学理及翻译实践上的启迪，从而给翻译专业的莘莘学子及相关教育工作者一份深入浅出的现场指导案卷。

目录

Contents

目录

Contents

罗选民序

Foreword by Luo Xuanmin

赵彦春教授请我给他的三字经英译本写序，我欣然接受。因为，我了解他的知识结构，相信他的中英文功底，更欣赏他的学术底蕴。

三字经是中华民族珍贵的文化遗产，与百家姓、千字文并称为三大国学启蒙读物，也是早期传教士介绍中国文化之首选。它短小精悍，朗朗上口，内容涵盖历史、天文、地理、道德以及一些民间传说。全文虽然不足两千字，但文字内涵丰富，典故琳琅。自 19 世纪以来，三字经英译本不少，但能兼顾『音』『形』『义』三方面的译本却很少。赵彦春教授敢为人先，在这方面做出了大胆的尝试。他以三个英文单词来对译汉语的三个字，在音节和押韵方面都力求做到丝丝入扣，形神兼顾。

我们先看他译本中的第一节：人之初，性本善。性相近，习相远。Man on earth / Good at birth / The same nature / Varies on nurture.

翻译采用 aabb 的押韵，第一二行，三个英文单词均为单音节词，用来对应三字一句的原文，吟咏起来，节拍都可达到一致。在三四行的结尾，分别用『nature』来对应『性』，用『nurture』来对应『习』不仅押韵合辙，而且词义也对应。四行的前两行为无动词小句，最后一行才出现动词，故语句之间衔接紧密，意义通贯，可谓是妙笔生花。类似的例子，在译本中屡见不鲜，如第二节中的『教之道，贵以专』，其英译便是『To teach well / You deeply dwell』。字字推敲，环环相扣，可见译者用力之深。

汉英对照之外，还有英汉注解，这恐怕是该译本的又一特色。对中国人来说，是学习英文的教材；对西方人来说，是学习中国语言进而学习中国文化的范本，具有『举一反三』的效力。

由于英文翻译紧扣原文每行三字的定制，这必然需要灵活

调变。翻译不只需要理性，也需要直觉的感性。领悟力很重要。甚至还需要偶尔的跳跃性思维，大胆摆脱原文束缚。但也正如舞者『台上一分钟，台下十年功』那样，要舞得漂亮，先要练好基本功，练好保持平衡的技法。这样在躲闪腾挪之时才不致跌倒。但是，正因为变通，译文中难免有一些看似『欠额翻译』的地方。比如『教不严，师之惰』翻译成『What's a teacher? /A strict preacher』，显然没有将原文内涵完全表现出來。不过，翻译只能如此，这是其『易』的本质所决定的，翻译不是字词的对等而是效果的对等。再参照前两行『What's a father?/A good teacher』，不难发现其语义并没有丢失，而且四行之间，竟是巧接妙合，一气贯通。与原文相比照，此译虽有『欠额』却是等效的。这可以看作是译者的技术处理。翻译是一个无限逼近的过程，我相信译者在今后的重版过程中还会不断地提升译文水平。我喜欢赵彦春教授的译本，并大力推荐之。是为序。

罗选民于清华园　2016 年 6 月 16 日

杨炳钧序

Foreword by Yang Bingjun

赵彦春教授是六零后，与他未曾谋面的学者大多以为他是位有着相当年纪的老者，原因是他的著作中所透露出来的功底之深厚、言辞之尖锐非常人所能及。平时有幸与赵教授谈译论道，而今蒙赵教授厚爱，希望我给他即将出版的英韵三字经作个序。受宠若惊之余，我开始反复咀嚼赵教授的译文。经过消化吸收，加上思量再三，我从三个方面来谈谈体会，权且为序。

第一，三字经影响深远，相关译文不少，而译好实在不容易。如果依照南宋学者王应麟（1223—1296）为最初的创作者这个说法，那么三字经已有七八百年的历史。该作品文字简练、三字成韵、朗朗上口，内容包括中国传统的教育、历史、天文、地理、伦理、道德等诸多方面，一问世即广为流传，成为优秀的儿童启蒙识字教材、文化教育材料和学习国学的入门读物。章炳麟曾说：『若所以诏小子者，则今之教科书，固弗如三字经远甚。』

明代以来，三字经不仅在国内广为流传，还被翻译为多种文字，远涉重洋到遥远的异国他乡播撒中国文化。据研究，世界上最早的三字经译本是意大利人罗明坚（Michele Ruggieri, 1543—1607）完成的拉丁文译本。罗明坚于1579年来到澳门学习中文，1581年开始着手翻译三字经。另外，英国人马礼逊（Robert Morrison, 1782—1834）、美国传教士裨治文（Elijah Coleman Bridgman, 1801—1861）、法国学者儒莲（Stanislas Julien, 1797—1873）、德裔英籍传教士欧德理（Ernest Johann Eitel, 1838—1908）等都曾翻译过三字经，对该作品的流传起着重要作用。虽然三字经已有很多译本，但从汉学家、华人乃至国内学者所翻译的情况看，要把这本书译好并非易事。

第二，译本比较是评价翻译的一种有效手段。要对一个译

本进行评价，仅从译本本身来谈缺乏基准，难免有失偏颇，与其他译本相比较会更客观公正。以下我们选取一个有较大影响的译本，拿来与赵彦春的译本进行简单比较。

在众多汉学家的译本中，翟理斯（Herbert Giles, 1845—1935）的译本影响较大。翟理斯曾经担任英国驻华使馆翻译，1897 年全票当选剑桥大学第二任汉学教授。1873 年，翟理斯出版了第一部汉英译作两首中国诗（*Two Chinese Poems*），其中包括无韵体三字经英译本；1910 年推出三字经重译本。翟理斯三字经英译本采用英汉对照的方式编排，每个汉字都注了音，还标明了音调。翟理斯根据许慎的说文对每一个汉字的结构、偏旁、部首等进行了分析，对诗文中涉及的历史、文化、典故也进行了介绍。作为一位优秀的英语诗人，翟理斯对三字经的翻译却缺少了本应保留的节奏韵律，虽然他对每一个汉字的发音都做了一个语音补偿，希望译文读者可以欣赏到原文本的韵律，但结果是既没有原文本句子的工整性，也没有把原文的韵律用英语翻译出来。或许是因为该译本的目的是教授汉语，它更像是一本汉语学习教材。例如，三字经开篇的几句话翟理斯是这样翻译的：

人之初（Jen chih chu）（Man arrive beginning）

Men at their birth;

性本善（Hsing pên shan）（Nature root good）

are naturally good.

性相近（Hsing hsiang chin）（Nature mutual near）

Their natures are much the same;

习相远（Hsi hsiang yüan）（Practice mutual far）

their habits become widely different.

相比之下，赵彦春的译文与翟理斯等众多译者的大为不同，概括起来包括以下六个特点：

一、目的明确，译境极高。三字经虽然是经典，但其创作目的主要是用来识字、广开见闻、介绍中华文明史、传播意识形态等。由于既要用来识字，又有非常丰富的具有文化内涵的内容，用其他文化背景下发展起来的语言来翻译时很难顾全，不易兼备。赵彦春的译文从总体上看，翻译目标明确，有与众不同的翻译境界。整个译文语言朴实而不平淡，流畅自然，深入浅出，情真意切。相信英文读者也能随着节拍摇头晃脑地吟诵起来。

二、对仗工整，韵律得当。三字经原文读起来朗朗上口，现今有些小学低年级学生都能一口气背诵下来。不少译者在这方面下了很大功夫，有些还尝试不拘一格，比如翟理斯的注音法试图最大程度地保留原文的韵律。但结果是要么译文的阅读被频繁打断，没有连续性；要么只能部分有韵律，美感不足；要么有韵律，而译语读者却难以理解或者应用。而赵彦春的译文是照应原作三字韵文的三词格偶韵体，节奏适当，朗朗上口。例如：

人之初，性本善。性相近，习相远。

Man on earth / Good at birth / The same nature / Varies on nurture.

勤有功，戏无益。戒之哉，宜勉力。

Good is diligence / Poor is negligence / Trials you breast / Work with zest.

三、用词精妙，锦上添花。译者未必首先是作家，但如果译者在选词择句上有创新，那么译作的效果未必逊于原作。如果外界环境适当，那么译作超过原作也未尝不可。赵彦春的译

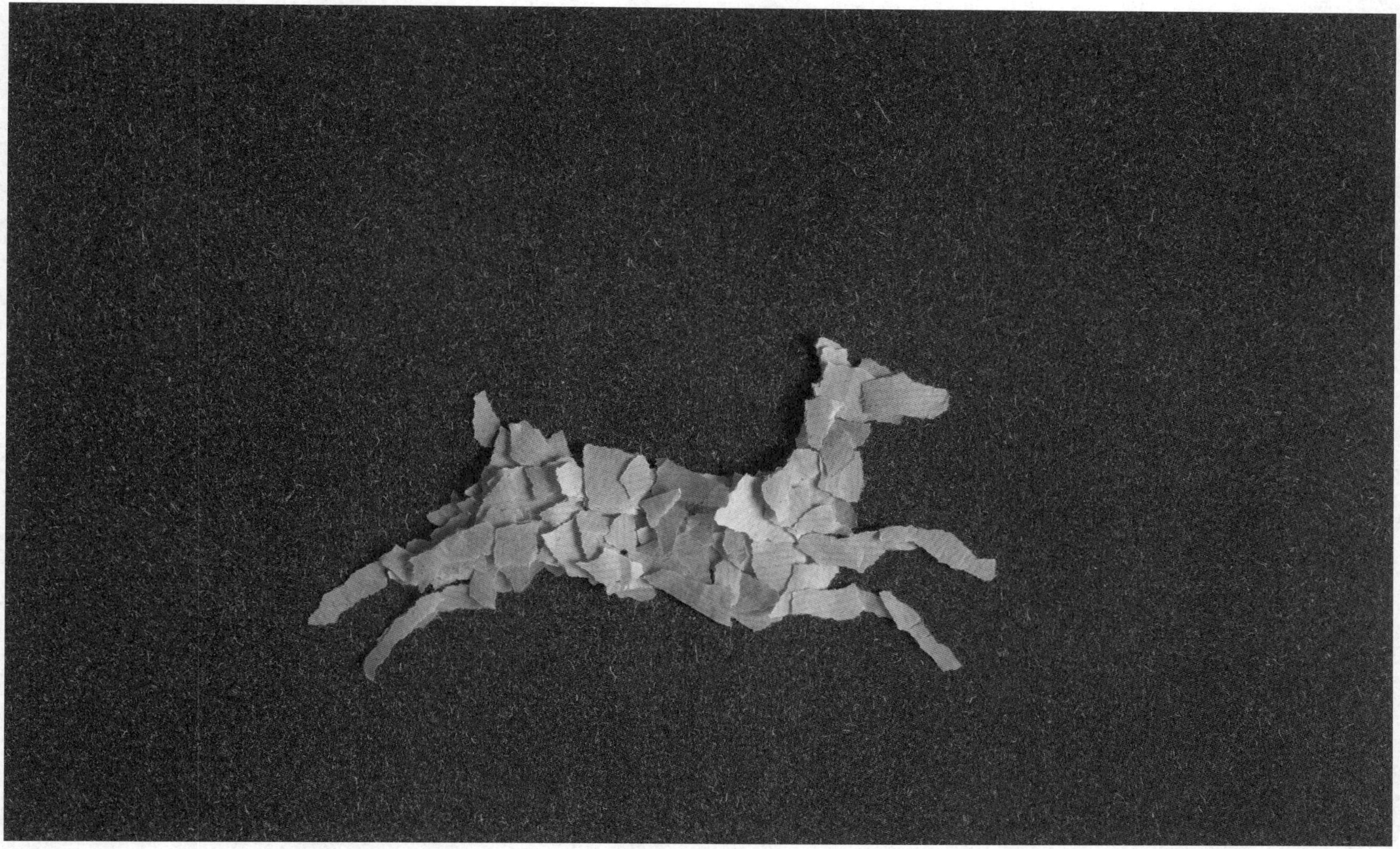

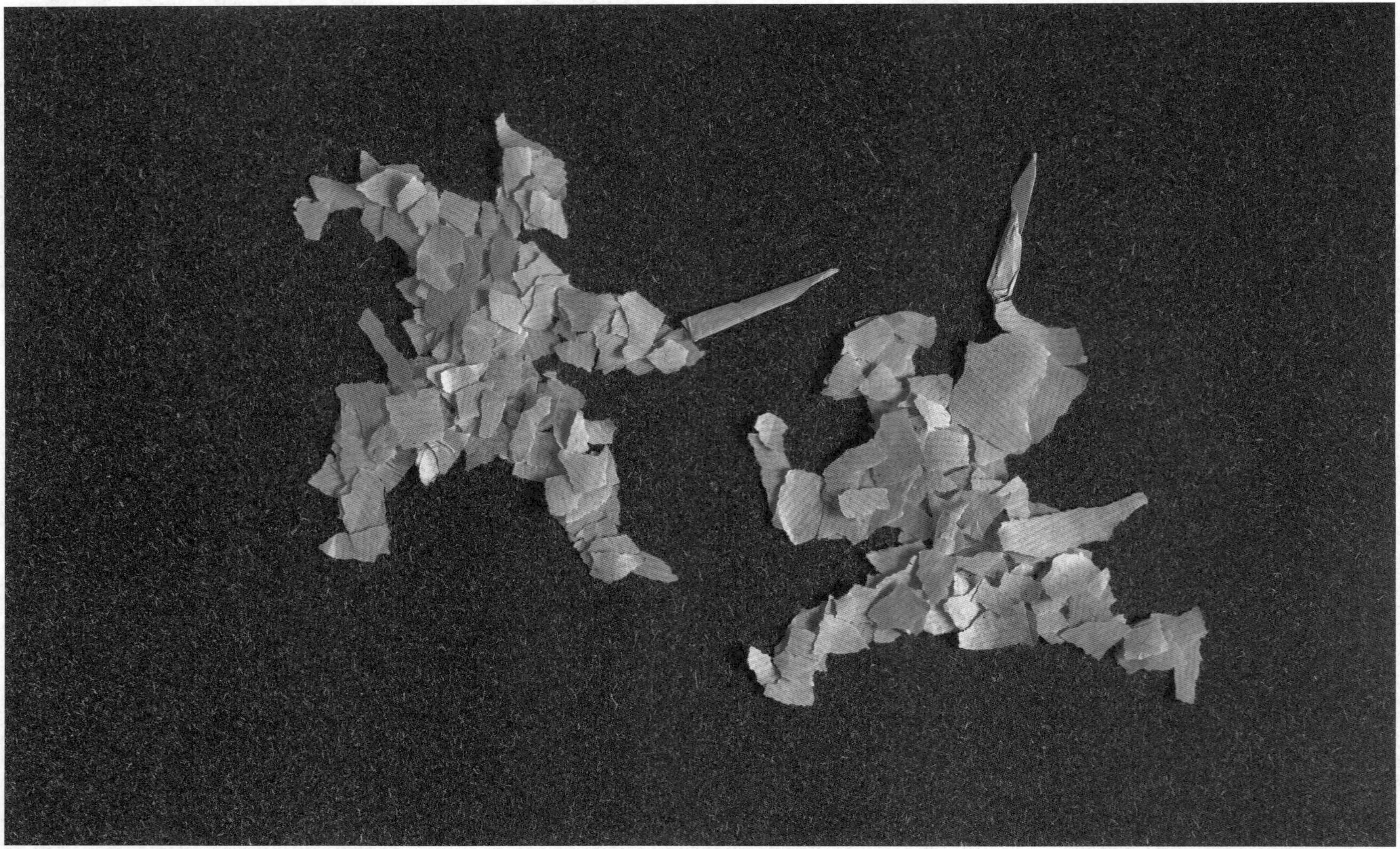

文中有不少词用得特别生动自然，让人不免感到英语语言的丰富内涵不亚于汉语，例如第八行的 dwell 一词。

苟不教，性乃迁。教之道，贵以专。

With no education / There'd be aberration / To teach well / You deeply dwell.

四、语言简洁，美感不失。做到用词简单而寓意丰富是一种语言使用的很高的境界，一般的功底和感悟是难以达成的。这类译文，懂点英语的人似乎一读都会，可在看到译文之前能想得到类似表达的人却寥寥无几。例如：

首孝悌，次见闻，知某数，识某文。

Stress piety more / Than your lore / Learn some numeracy / Know some literacy.

五、比照名译，更胜一筹。许多地方的译文令人叹为观止，如果与已经流传久远的译文进行比较，你就不得不叹服赵彦春的译文。当然，这或许正是『后浪推前浪』的真实写照。例如：

一而十，十而百，百而千，千而万。

One to ten / A hundred then / One thousand more / Ten thousand afore.（赵彦春译）

Units and tens,tens and hundreds,hundreds and thousands, thousands and tens of thousands.（翟理斯译）

显然，赵彦春的译文不仅把数数的累积特点译了出来，与翟理斯的译文相比节奏和韵律感都更强。其中，to, then, more和afore 几个词更表现出一种内在的运动感。

六、注释独特，促进理解。很多译文要么仅选取部分来注解，要么注释本身严重打乱阅读的顺畅性，要么注解偏深或偏浅，影响了对原文意义的传递。赵彦春译文的注释方法无碍于

原文之美感的传递，因为先把原文按节来翻译，然后每节下面有简短的偏重含义的解释。如果读者了解原文的相关背景，那他可以直接跳到下一节，不需要读注释。如果不了解，也可以以节为单位稍作停顿，先看注解。也就是说，读者完全可以根据自己的情况和自己的需要自行决定是否阅读注释部分。例如，其中关于『三才』和『三光』的注释如下：

大家还应该学习一些基本知识，比如什么叫三才？三才指的是天、地、人三个元素。什么叫三光呢？三光就是太阳、月亮、星星。

And one should know some rudiments, such as what we call tri-vitals, Heaven, Earth, Man, and what we call three luminaries or lights, Sun, Moon and Stars.

第三，与众多翻译一样，典籍翻译也要明确三个问题，即原作像什么，为什么译以及翻译给谁看，也即原作地位、翻译目的与读者对象问题。

三字经原作虽然被当作识字读本，但该著作并非仅仅是儿童读物。可以说，原作老少皆宜，研学兼可。如果仅仅把该作品当作儿童读物，小看它的艺术性和文学性，那么翻译出来的译文虽然简单易懂，但很可能就丧失了文学性，更不可能有艺术性了。而如果受其经典性的影响而非得要用深奥的语词进行翻译，那么译文又可能会丧失可读性。译文兼顾这两方面很难，但并非做不到。赵彦春的译本就是明证。

可以说，几乎人类的每一项活动都是有目的的，或者说有指向性的。三字经翻译出来之后，我们并不希望译文只藏在亭台楼阁 而是要让有译语背景的人尽可能认识它，受它感化。作为一种创作活动，翻译既要感人，又得化人，即感化人。如果

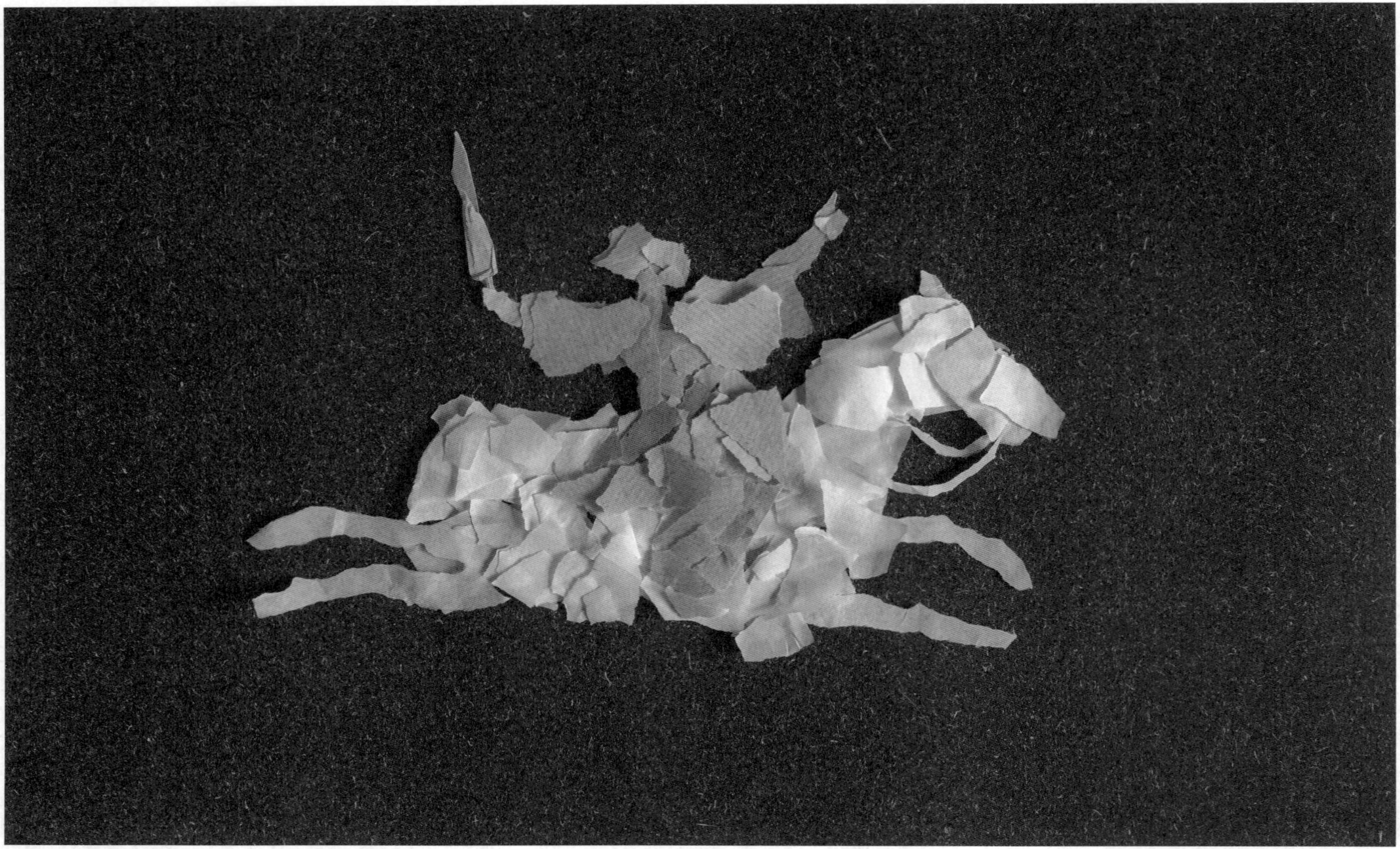

原作能感化众生，而译作仅仅是个科研成果，让读者得不到感化，那么该翻译活动的目的便没有达到，意义也荡然无存。依我看，赵彦春的译本能够发挥感化众人的作用，因为该译本具备了感化他人的作品的众多特质。

翻译给谁看表面看似简单，实质上很难决断。让作品有最大可能的读者群仅仅是每一个作者的美好愿望，不过作者的主体性受限很小，可以比较明确地设定读者对象群体，有所取舍。而除了翻译当代作品外，译者一般不太可能与原作者有直接面对面交流的机会，如果缺乏相关记载，那就难以确定作者所指的读者对象。这样一来，译给谁看往往可以自由发挥。译给甲看，乙可能不满意；译给乙看，丙可能不满意。这类骑虎难下是常态。如果能够巧妙地通过译语尽可能充分地表达出源语的音美、形美和意美，那么就无所谓读者对象了。随读者去理解，任由读者阐释，因为这个时候的译文本身已经是一种创作。赵彦春的译本给了我这样的感觉，其本身就是一种创作，即等同于创作的自足性文本。

杨炳钧　谨识　2016 年 11 月 11 日

Education

教

人之初，性本善。性相近，习相远。

Man on earth, Good at birth. The same nature Varies on nurture.

A child should have proper education.
If one does not do well,
what will become of him when he is grown up?

人在太初或刚出生时其本性都是善良的，由于后天成长环境、教育背景不同，性情也就有了各种各样的差别。

苟不教，性乃迁。教之道，贵以专。

37 With no education, There'd be aberration. To teach well, You deeply dwell.

If a child is not properly taught,
he may go astray.
In education, what is important is to be focused,
dwelling on key points.

对孩子如果不进行适当的教育，其本性就会发生变化。说到教育，最关键的问题就是要专心一致，精讲要义而不厌其烦。

昔孟母，
择邻处。
子不学，
断机杼。

Then Mencius' mother Chose her neighbor. At Mencius' sloth, She cut th' cloth.

In the Warring States period,
Mencius' mother moved three times
for better environment for her son.
Mencius once played truant,
and she cut the cloth to show her seriousness and
the consequences of interrupted learning.

战国时期，孟子的母亲为使孟子有个良好的学习环境曾三次搬家。有一次孟子逃学，孟母就割断织布机上的布，以此表明事情的严重性和中断学习的后果。

41

教

Education

窦燕山，有义方。教五子，名俱扬。

Dough by name Fulfilled his aim. His five sons Became famous ones.

In the Five Dynasties and
Ten Kingdoms period, there was a man,
Dough by name, from the Swallow Hills.
He founded a private school, hired famous teachers,
and managed well in having his children taught.
All his five sons passed Grand Test
or the Imperial Examinations as it is often called,
and lived very successful lives.

五代十国时期，有个燕山人，名叫窦禹钧。他创办私塾，延聘名师，教子有方。他的五个儿子都科举成名，很有成就。

养不教，父之过。教不严，师之惰。

45 What's a father? A good teacher. What's a teacher? A strict preacher.

It is not enough to provide children
with food and clothing. Education is important.
To rear children without giving them
good education is a father's fault;
a teacher is considered lazy if he is not strict
with the children he teaches.

养育儿女，仅仅供其吃穿，而不进行良好的教育，那便是做父亲的过错。教育为本，但是只教育，而不严格要求，那就是做老师的没有尽到职责了。

子不学，非所宜。幼不学，老何为？

An unschooled child Will grow wild. A young loafer, An old loser!

A child should have proper education.
If one does not do well,
what will become of him when he is grown up?

小孩子应该好好学习。一个人小时候如果不好好学习，到老的时候能有什么用呢？

玉不琢，
不成器。
人不学，
不知义。

49 No jade crude Shows craft good. Unless you learn, Brute you'll turn.

If jade is not honed and carved,
it will not be a fine piece of art;
if one does not receive education,
he will not be a gentleman,
and will not be something.

璞玉不经打磨，便不会成为精美的艺术品；人要是不学习，就不懂得人情礼节，也就不能成为有用之才。

为人子，方少时。亲师友，习礼仪。

Son of man, Mature you can. Teacher or peer, Hold them dear.

As children, you will grow up like Son of Man.
While young, you should approach
and requite your models like teachers and friends,
and learn good manners from them.

作为儿女，或如人子，终会长大成人。在成长过程中应学会亲近师友，当心存感激，不要轻慢无礼，要学一些为人处世的礼节。

51

教

Education

香九龄，
能温席。
孝于亲，
所当执。

Hsiang, at nine, Warmed bedding fine. Follow this one, This filial son.

There was a boy named Hsiang (Huang Xiang)
in the Eastern Han Dynasty,
who knew how to show kindness to his parents, nine years old as he was.
He warmed bedding for his father in winter.
One should do like this, to be a filial son.

东汉时，有个叫黄香的，九岁时就懂得孝顺父母，比如他冬天给父亲暖热被窝。这种行为是每个孝顺父母的人都应该实行和效仿的。

融四岁，能让梨。弟于长，宜先知。

55 Aged four years, Rong proffered pears. Bear in mind: Fraternally be kind.

And in the Han Dynasty,
Rong (Kong Rong), Confucius' descendant,
offered his pears to his elder brother although he was only four.
Everyone should learn this kind of respect for affinity.

汉代时，孔子的后人孔融年仅四岁就知道把梨让给哥哥吃。这种谦让的态度和友爱兄长的美德，是每个人从小就应该知道的。

首孝悌，次见闻。知某数，识某文。

57 Stress piety more Than your lore. Learn some numeracy, Know some literacy.

Piety (loving parents and brothers)
is more important than knowledge.
As for knowledge, one should learn some numeracy and literacy.

孝敬父母、爱护兄弟是首要的，其次才是知识。至于知识，大家要学点算术和语文。

Knowledge

知

我国采用十进位数制：一到十是基本数字，然后依次为一百、一千、一万……以此数制可以无穷地计算下去。

一而十，
十而百，
百而千，
千而万。

One to ten, A hundred then,
One thousand more, Ten thousand afore.

Decimalism is adopted in China:
one to ten is primary,
the next is one hundred,
then one thousand, ten thousand, and so on.
All computations can be done with this.

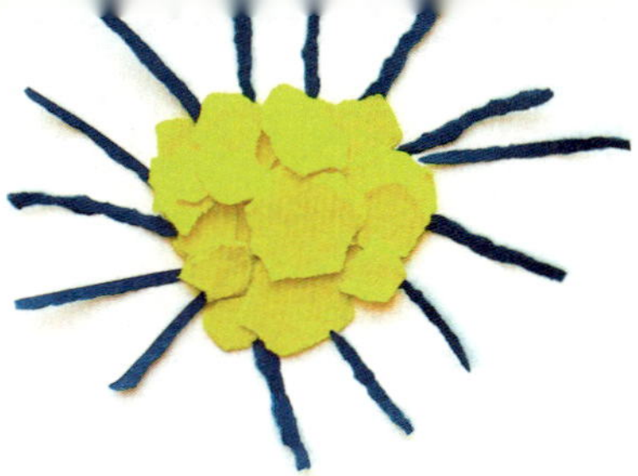

三才者，天地人。三光者，日月星。

大家还应该学习一些基本知识，比如什么叫三才？三才指的是天、地、人三个元素。什么叫三光呢？三光就是太阳、月亮、星星。

Tri-vitals, of worth: Man, heaven, earth;
Tri-lights, a boon: Sun, stars, moon.

And one should know some rudiments,
such as what we call tri-vitals, or three elements,
that is, Heaven, Earth, Man,
and what we call tri-lights or three luminaries,
that is, Sun, Moon and Stars.

63

知

Knowledge

64

人与人之间应该遵守的三个行为准则是什么呢？就是君王与臣子之间要合乎义理，父母子女之间要相亲相爱，夫妻之间要和和美美。

三纲者，君臣义。父子亲，夫妇顺。

Three Tenets always: Subject Lord obeys;
Child Father reveres; Wife Man endears.

What are the three tenets one should always follow?
The king or emperor should be obeyed by his subjects,
the father should be revered by his children,
and the man loved by his wife.

曰春夏，
曰秋冬。
此四时，
运不穷。

春、夏、秋、冬叫做四时，即一年分为四个季节。这四个季节按照一定的规律交替运行，春去夏来，秋去冬来，循环往复，以至无穷。

Spring and summer, Autumn and winter.
These four seasons Cycle with reasons.

We have four seasons:
spring, summer, fall, and winter.
They alternate according to a certain law,
round by round,
never to end.

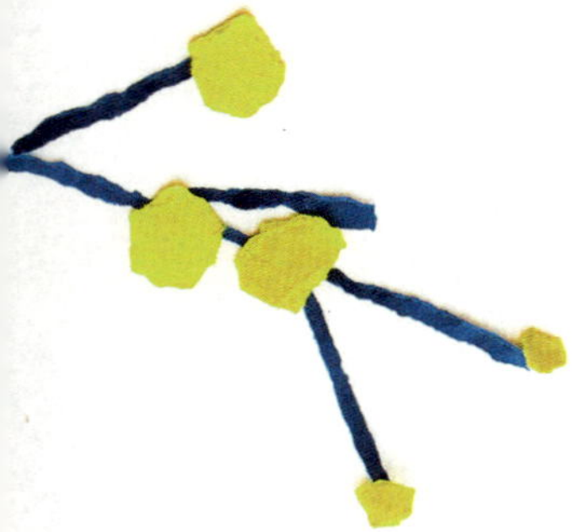

东、南、西、北，这叫做四方，是四个方向。这四个方位是相对的，必须有个中心位置才能确定各个方位。

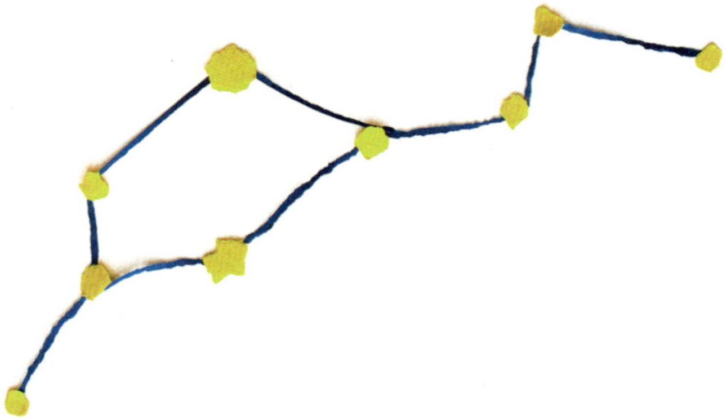

曰南北，曰西东。此四方，应乎中。

South, north, west, 'N east, we quest.
These four ways Upon center gaze.

We have four ways or directions called east, west, south, and north.
These four ways are reciprocal, determined by a central position.

所谓五行，指的是金、木、水、火、土。五行用来指称宇宙间的各种抽象概念，可看作五大表征。五行根据一、二、三、四、五的数理，相生相克。

曰水火，
木金土。
此五行，
本乎数。

Water, fire, behold, Earth, wood, gold.
These five materials Accord to numerals.

The so-called five elements are gold, wood, water, fire, and earth. These represent various abstract ideas humans have of the cosmos. The five elements we may understand as five representations. They form a system of checks and balances depending on the combination and function of the numerals, that is, one, two, three, four, and five.

69

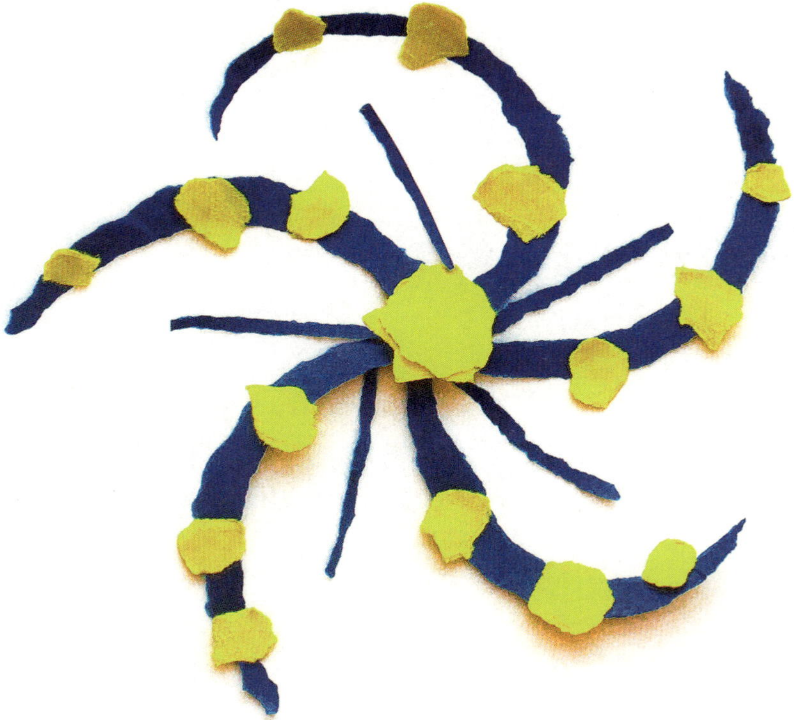

知

Knowledge

十干者，甲至癸。十二支，子至亥。

The Ten Trunks Are great chunks.
The Twelve Wings Are good things.

「十干」指「天干」的十个要素，即甲、乙、丙、丁、戊、己、庚、辛、壬、癸；「十二支」指「地支」的十二个要素，即子、丑、寅、卯、辰、巳、午、未、申、酉、戌、亥。「天干」与「地支」两两配对，组成循环往复的「六十干支」。

The Ten Trunks are Crust (jia), Creep (yi),
Flame (bing), Strong (ding), Rank (wu),
Rise (ji), Wait (geng), New (xin), Bear (ren), Rear (gui);
The Twelve Wings are Babe (zi), Sprout (chou),
Spread (yin), Grow (mao), Mature (chen), Prime (si),
Ripe (wu), Taste (wei), Grown (shen),

Old (you), Sear (xu), End (hai).
The combination of two elements respectively from the trunk and wing systems makes a recursive sexagenary cycle, also known as Trunks-and-Wings, that is, a cyclic numeral system of 60 combinations of the Ten Trunks and the Twelve Wings.

地球围着太阳转；太阳围着银河系转。『黄道』指地球围绕太阳运行的轨道，『赤道』指地球中央那条假想的与地轴垂直的大圆圈。

曰黄道，
日所躔。
曰赤道，
当中权。

The Ecliptic line, The Zodiacal Sign.
And the Equator Circling the center.

The earth revolves around the sun,
and the sun revolves around the Milky Way.
The track of the revolution of the earth is called ecliptic,
and the imaginary circle vertical to
the earth's axis is called equator.

地球的赤道地带，气候特别炎热，属热带；从赤道向南向北两个方向，气温逐渐变低。我们国家地处地球的东北边。

赤道下，温暖极。我中华，在东北。

Nowhere is hotter Than the equator.
China, the greatest, Lies in Northeast.

Along the equator, it is the hottest,
and this is the tropical zone.
Temperature drops gradually south and north of the equator.
China is northeast on the earth.

我国气候冷暖匀称，有霜期和露期。右边是高原，左边是大海。

寒燠均，霜露改。右高原，左大海。

Temperature fitting you, There's frosty dew.
Right, plateaus stand; Left, seas expand.

China has a mild temperature,
with frost and dew.
On the right there are plateaus,
and on the left there are great seas.

中国有许多河流，直接流入大海的有长江、黄河、淮河和济水，这四条大河是中国河流的代表。

曰江河，
曰淮济。
此四渎，
水之纪。

Long and River, Clara and Phora.
These rivers four All along outpour.

China has many rivers.
The four representatives, the Long (the Yangtze River),
the River (the Yellow River),
the Level (the Huai River),
and the Phora (the Ji River) flow into the sea.

中国多山，有五大名山，总称『五岳』，即东岳泰山、西岳华山、中岳嵩山、南岳衡山、北岳恒山。

曰岱华，
嵩恒衡。
此五岳，
山之名。

Arch, Flora, Tower, Scale, and Ever!
These high mountains Are five chieftains.

China has five famous representative mountains, called Five Mounts-Arch (Mount Tai) in the east, Flora (Mount Hua) in the west, Tower (Mount Song) at the center, Scale (Mount Heng) in the south, and Ever (Mount Heng) in the north.

79

知

Knowledge

曰士农，
曰工商。
此四民，
国之良。

中国人口众多，为世界之最。官员、农民、工人和商人称为『四民』，这是社会的重要组成部分。

Officials and farmers, Merchants and workers,
These four great, Maintain the State.

China has the largest population in the world.
Officials, farmers, workers,
and merchants are the mainstay of the society.

曰仁义，
礼智信。
此五常，
不容紊。

为人处世应当牢记仁、义、礼、智、信这五种不变的法则，这样社会才能稳定祥和。

Grace, justice, courtesy, Wisdom, and fidelity.
Good order derive From Constants Five.

Everyone should bear in mind what we call Constants Five-grace, justice, courtesy, wisdom, and fidelity. Only the constants are kept can the society be stable and peaceful.

地所生，
有草木。
此植物，
遍水陆。

地球上有花草，有树木，这些属于植物，陆上、水里到处都有。

Earth makes good Grass and wood.
These plants command Water and land.

There grow grass, flowers, and trees on earth.
There are plants everywhere on land and in water.

中国的动物类包括虫、鱼、鸟和兽。有的能在天空飞，有的能在陆地走，有的能在水里游。

有虫鱼，
有鸟兽。
此动物，
能飞走。

Fishes and birds, Worms and herds.
These creatures cry, Run or fly.

Worms, fishes, birds,
and herds make the fauna of China.
Some can fly in the sky,
some can walk over the land,
and some can swim in water.

稻子、小麦、豆类、小米、玉米和高粱是中国人的主食。

稻粱菽，麦黍稷。此六谷，人所食。

Rice, sorghum, beans, Wheat, millet, corns.
These crops main Our life sustain.

The staple food of the Chinese people is from such crops as rice, wheat, beans, corns, millet, and sorghum.

在动物中有马、牛、羊、鸡、狗和猪，驯化而来，这叫六畜。

马牛羊，
鸡犬豕。
此六畜，
人所饲。

Horses, sheep, cows, Chickens, dogs, sows.
These six breeds A husbandman feeds.

Horses, cows, sheep, chickens, dogs,
and pigs are six breeds that have been domesticated.

曰喜怒，
曰哀惧。
爱恶欲，
七情具。

喜、怒、哀、惧、爱、恶、欲，合起来叫七情。这是人类与生俱来的七种感情。

Say anger, gladness, Say fear, sadness,
Hate, greed, love. Seven feelings above.

Anger, happiness, fear, sadness, love, hate, and greed are seven leading emotions that humans are born with.

青赤黄，
及黑白。
此五色，
目所识。

青色、黄色、赤色、黑色和白色，是最常见、最重要的五种颜色，是人眼所能够识别的。

Green, red, yellow, Black ’n white follow.
Five colors vie, Wakening the eye.

Green, yellow, red, black, and white are the five main colors traditionally deemed important by the Chinese people. They are discernible to the naked eye.

我们能够用味觉分辨出来的味道，有酸、甜、苦、辣、咸这五种。

酸苦甘，及辛咸。此五味，口所含。

Sour, bitter, sweet, Hot 'n salty meet.
These tastes five Make palates alive.

There are five tastes perceptible to the tongue, namely, sour, bitter, hotness, sweet, and salty.

我们用鼻子可以闻出的气味，主要有五种，即羊膻味、烧焦味、香味、鱼腥味和腐朽味。

膻焦香，
及腥朽。
此五臭，
鼻所嗅。

Muttony, burnt, balmy, Fishy, and moldy,
These smells five Make noses alive.

There are five main smells perceptible to the nose, namely, muttony, burnt, balmy, fishy, and moldy.

我国古人根据材料把乐器分为八种，即匏瓜、黏土、皮革、木块、石头、金属、丝线与竹子，统称为『八音』。

匏土革，
木石金，
丝与竹，
乃八音。

Gourd, leather, clay, Wood we play,
Stone, metal, bamboo, And strings, too.

The ancient Chinese people
made a division of eight musical instruments
according to materials they were made of,
namely, gourd, clay, leather, wood, stone, metal, strings,
and bamboo, called “musical eight”.

曰平上，
曰去入。
此四声，
宜调协。

Level, and bounce, Fall, and in-nounce.
These four tones For tuned phones.

中国古人把说话声音的声调分为平、上、去、入四种。这四个单音应该和谐悦耳。

Ancient Chinese spoke with four tones:
level, bounce, fall, and in-nounce,
and these four tones should be in tune.

高曾祖，父而身，身而子，子而孙。

由高祖父生曾祖父，曾祖父生祖父，祖父生父亲，父亲生我本身，我生儿子，儿子再生孙子。

Grand, great-grand, great-great-grand Father,
myself, and Children, and grandchildren
All are kinsmen.

Greater grandparents (great-great-grand) beget great-grandparents, great-grandparents beget grandparents, grandparents beget father, and father begets son, etc.

自子孙，至玄曾。乃九族，人之伦。

从高祖父到曾孙称为『九族』。这『九族』代表着家族血统的承续关系。

Now great-grand, and His son, great-great-grand.
There're generations nine, A genealogical line.

From great-grand (great-great-grandfather) to great-grand (great-great-grandchildren), there are all together nine generations, forming a kindred genealogical line.

父子恩，夫妇从。兄则友，弟则恭。

父子有恩情，夫妻要和顺，兄对弟友爱，弟对兄尊敬。

Father loves son; Man-wife is one.
Brothers are bland, Hand in hand.

A father should love his children and be loved by them,
man and wife should be harmonious,
and brothers should be kind
-the older takes care of the younger
and the younger shows respect to the older.

长幼序，友与朋。君则敬，臣则忠。

社会生活中应当有长幼尊卑的次序；君主爱护臣子，以民为本，民则敬仰君主。

Senior to young, The ethical rung.
Lord loves subjects, And enjoys respects.

There should be an ethical rung
-the old should be given priority;
If a king loves his subjects,
the latter will respect him and be loyal to him.

前面提到的十义是人人都应遵守并广为宣传的，千万不能违背。

此十义，人所同。当师叙，勿违背。

This you remember For every member.
This you obey For every day.

The above-mentioned moral principles should be borne in mind and be told to others, and should never be breached.

中国古代有五种孝服，分别是斩衰、齐衰、大功、小功和缌麻。

斩齐衰，大小功。至缌麻，五服终。

Cuts and completes, Merits and feats,
And linen, too, For funeral blue.

There are five kinds of funeral garments in ancient China, that is, cuts (cut coarsely), completes (complete with all parts), merits (probably to commemorate the merits of the dead), feats (probably to commemorate the feats of the dead), and linen .

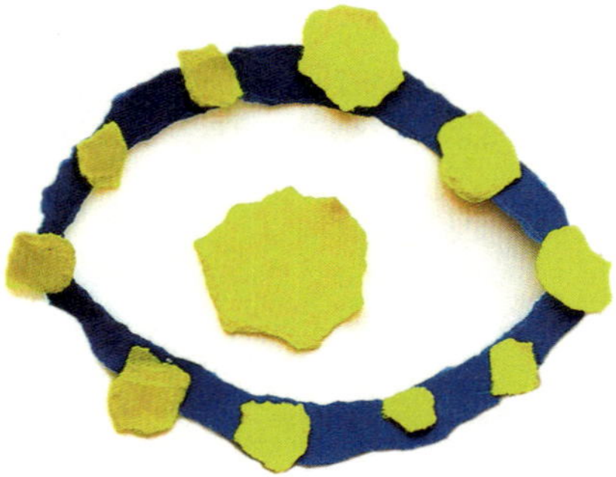

有古文，
大小篆。
隶草继，
不可乱。

Old characters, behold Seals, lesser 'n bold,
Square and cursive, Five scripts successive!

我国的文字演变出了古文、大篆、小篆、隶书、草书这五种主要形式。这些一定要认清楚，不可搞乱了。

Chinese script styles developed from old characters,
to bold seal, lesser seal, square, and cursive.
These styles should be distinguished each from the other.

Learning

若广学，
惧其繁。
但略说，
能知原。

To learn widely
Is seldom easy.
To study some,
Informed you become.

假如你想广泛地学习知识，实在是一件不容易的事情，但是如果大体涉猎，还是能够了解到许多基本道理的。

If you want to learn extensively, it is not an easy matter.
If you study generally, you'll become knowing,
with an acquisition of some basic facts.

礼乐射，

御书数。

古六艺，

今不具。

Rituals, calligraphy, shooting,
Music, mathematics, driving.
These six arts
Need devoted hearts.

Rituals, music, shooting, driving, calligraphy,
and mathematics are the six courses or
arts the ancient people were required to learn at school.
These arts are demanding,
and now very few people can master them all.

礼法、音乐、射箭、驾车、书法和算数是古代读书人的六门课程，统称『六艺』。六艺需全身心投入，到现在很少有人能同时具备了。

惟书学，人共遵。既识字，讲说文。

Calligraphy's the one
Neglected by none.
Words already learned,
Motivations are concerned.

Of the six arts, now only calligraphy is valued by everybody.
When one has learned enough characters,
it is necessary to inquire into the *Motivations of the Characters*.

在六艺中，现在只有书法还广受推崇。认识了一些汉字之后，你就可以去研究《说文解字》了。

凡训蒙，须讲究。
详训诂，明句读。

老师教导小学生，必须耐心认真，每句话都要详细解释，使之懂得断句，了解句子的起承转合。

While you teach,
Do deeply reach.
Go with explanation,
And guide punctuation.

As a teacher of children, you should reach deeply, carefully explain what a sentence means and teach them how to understand the cohesion and coherence of a text.

学习要有一个良好的开端，求学初期要打好基础，循序渐进，小学之后才可以读四书。

为学者，必有初。小学终，至四书。

Now to learn,
Make a turn.
From school nooks
To *Four Books*.

A learner should have a good beginning.
Only on a good foundation in primary school
can a learner proceed to the classics, i.e. the *Four Books*.

论语者，二十篇。群弟子，记善言。

Analects—the lections,
Has twenty sections.
Confucius and disciples
Gave off sparkles.

The Analects, consisting of twenty sections,
is a book of sparkling dialogues between Confucius and his disciples.

《论语》二十篇，记载的是孔子及弟子们之间的言论，皆是微言大义的警语。

孟子者，七篇止。讲道德，说仁义。

Mencius, the sutras,
Has seven chapters.
These are counsels
Of virtues 'n morals.

Mencius, named after the author,
is divided into seven chapters,
which are counsels of virtues and morals.

《孟子》这本书，孟轲所作，共分七篇。内容是关于品行修养、道德仁义等方面的言论。

中庸这本书的作者是孔子的孙子孔伋。书中讲的是中庸，即不偏、不变的意思。

作中庸，乃孔伋。
中不偏，庸不易。

The Golden Mean,
Great it's been.
Kong Jih, the scholar,
Is its author.

The Golden Mean was authored by Kong Jih,
grandson of Confucius,
which is about how to keep constant equilibrium.

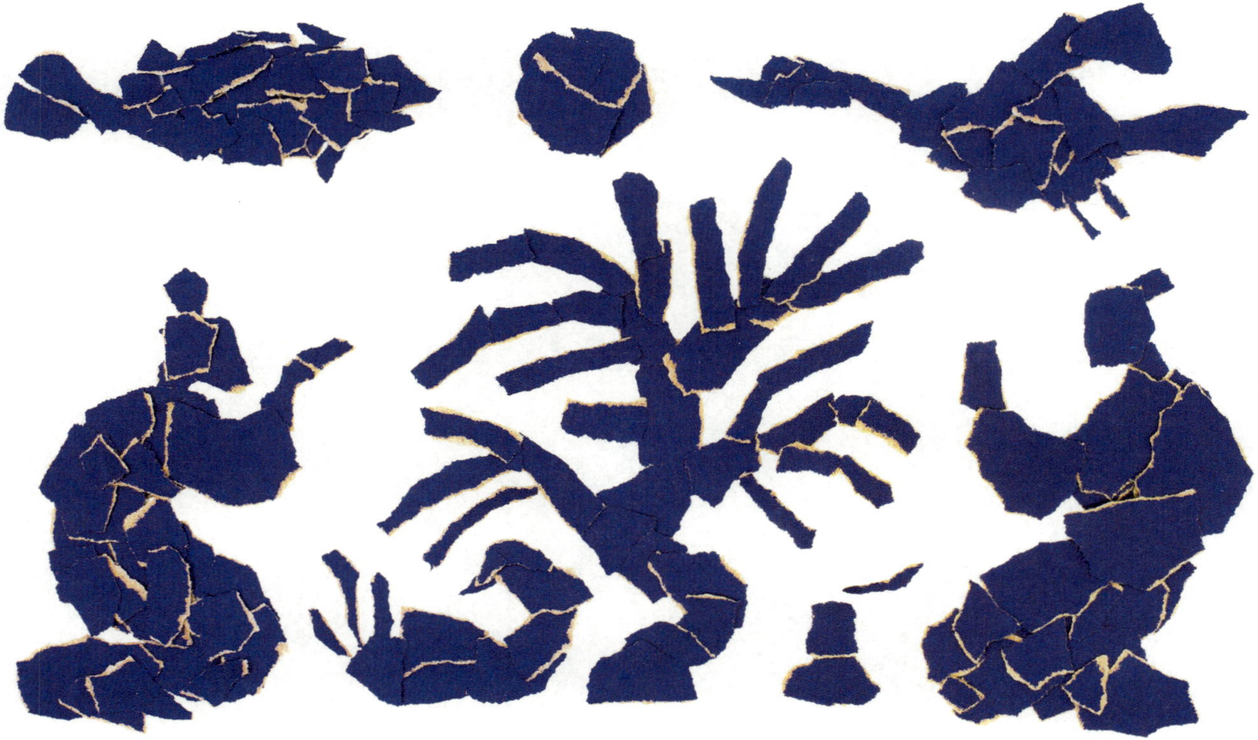

119

学

Learning

作大学，乃曾子。自修齐，至平治。

Great Learning, great,
Tsengcius did create:
From personal perfection
To national progression.

《大学》这本书的作者是孔子的弟子曾参。他提出了修齐平治的主张，具体是『修身齐家治国平天下』。

Great Learning was written by
one of Confucius' disciples by the name of Tsengcius,
who proposed the idea of personal perfection and national progression,
to be specific, self-perfection, family harmonizing,
state governing, and world pacification.

孝经通，四书熟。如六经，始可读。

先学了孝经中的道理，然后再把四书读熟了，这样就可以去读六经这样的经典了。

Piety learned ahead,
Four Books fully-read,
Six Classics now,
You should plough.

After you have learned
what is preached in *Piety* and get versed in *Four Books*,
you can proceed to plough through *Six Classics*.

诗书易，
礼春秋。
号六经，
当讲求。

诗、书、易、礼、春秋，再加上乐统称『六经』。这是中国古代儒家的经典，应当仔细阅读。

History, Changes, Odes,
Books of altitudes.
Spring 'n Fall, Rituals,
Books for perusals.

Odes (or called *Poems*), *History, Changes, Spring 'n Fall, Rituals,*
and *Music* are collectively called *Six Classics.*
These are important Confucian literatures to be read closely.

有连山，
有归藏，
有周易，
三易详。

连山、周易、归藏是我国古代的三部书，合称『三易』，『三易』用『卦』的形式来说明宇宙间万事万物的循环变化。

Book of Ranges,
Book of Changes,
Book of Retreat,
Detailed and great.

Book of Ranges, Book of Changes, Book of Retreat are three important books in Ancient China, collectively called three books of changes, in which divinatory symbols are used to predict the changes of things in the universe.

有典谟，
有训诰，
有誓命，
书之奥。

Canons, duties, plans,
Edicts, and bans,
And imperial mandates,
Are *History*'s aggregates.

书经包括立国的基本原则、治国计划、大臣义务、国君通告、起兵文告、国君命令等内容。

History includes state documents such as canons, duties, plans, edicts, oaths, bans, and imperial mandates.

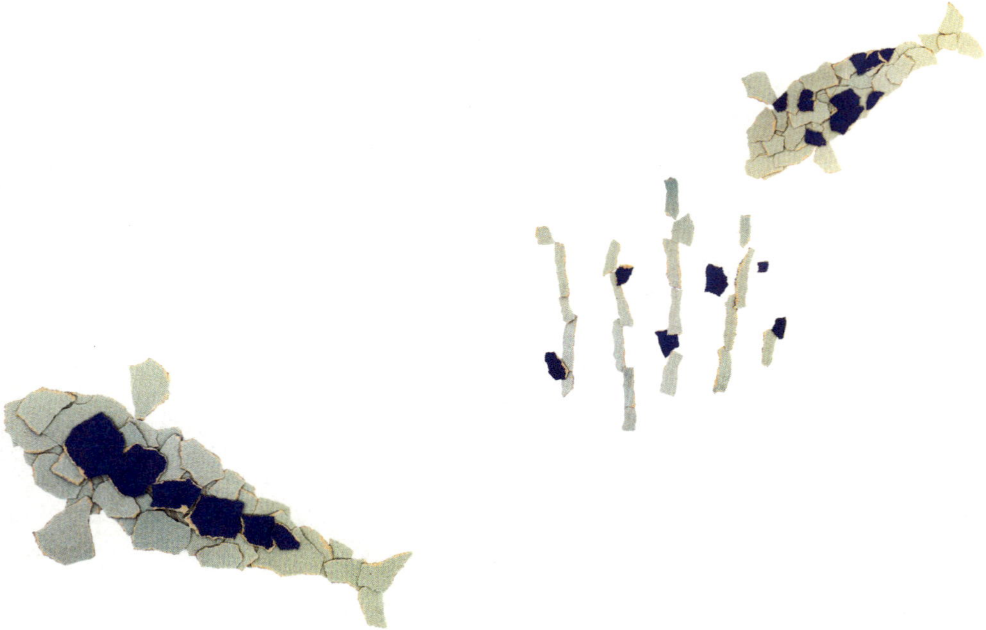

我周公，
作周礼。
着六官，
存治体。

Th' Prince of Chough
Did *Rituals* bestow.
Regimen he designed
And government defined.

周公制定了周礼，其中他设计了六宫的官制，规定了国家的体制。

The Prince of Chough wrote *Rituals*,
in which he designed the nuptial system of the crown and
defined the governmental system of the country.

大小戴，注礼记。述圣言，礼乐备。

The Days supplied
Rituals well clarified,
And paraphrased adages
Of those sages.

The Days, i.e. Day Deh the uncle and Day Shen the nephew, annotated *Rituals*, and illustrated the decrees, regulations, and etiquette rules of ancient times and paraphrased what had been written by the sages then.

戴德和戴圣叔侄二人整理并且注释了礼记，转述和阐扬了前代的典章制度和有关礼乐，阐明了圣贤的精辟言论。

曰国风，
曰雅颂。
号四诗，
当讽咏。

国风、大雅、小雅、颂，合称为『四诗』，构成诗经这部内容丰富、中国最早的诗歌总集。

The *Psalms*, say,
The *Chants*, say,
And those airs
Of various affairs.

The four collections, i.e. *Airs of the States*, *Psalms Major*, *Psalms Minor*, and *Chants* constitute *Poems* or *Book of Odes*, a rich resource of poems,the earliest collection in China.

随着周朝的衰落，诗经变得默默无闻了，在此情况下孔子撰写了春秋，以借古讽今，扬善去恶。

诗既亡，
春秋作。
寓褒贬，
别善恶。

When *Poems* perished,
Spring 'n Fall flourished,
Flogging what's lewd,
Praising what's good.

As the Chough House declined,
Poems or *Book of Odes* lost its popularity,
so Confucius compiled *Spring 'n Fall* to criticize the ill-doing,
and praise the well-being, of the society.

132

三传者，
有公羊，
有左氏，
有谷梁。

Companion authors three:
Tsuo Qiu-ming, and he
Who was Gongyang,
And another, Goo Liang.

The three companions to
Spring 'n Fall were those written by Gongyang
(Yang Gao or Gongyang Gao),
Tsuo Qiu-ming, and Goo Liang.

「三传」是解释春秋的三部书，指公羊高所著的公羊传、左丘明所著的左传和谷梁赤所著的谷梁传。

经既明，方读子。撮其要，记其事。

读完了这些经传，明白了其间的道理，就可以读子书了。由于子书很多，应该选择一些比较重要的来读，而且还要记住每一事件的要点。

Classics well read,
Study sophists ahead.
Make a list,
Get the gist.

After finishing the classics,
you can read sophistic essays.
Since there are so many such books,
you should make a list of important ones and
try to get the gist of each.

五子者，有荀扬。文中子，及老庄。

Five sophists then
Were great men:
Hsun, Wenchong, Yang
Lao and Tsuang.

五子所著的书，称为『子书』，所谓『五子』指荀子、扬子、文中子、老子和庄子。

The books written by five sophists are called sophistic books.
The five sophists refer to Hsuncius,
Yangcius, Wenchongcius, Laocius, and Tsuangcius.

经子通，读诸史。考世系，知终始。

经书和子书都读熟了之后，就可以读史书了。读史书时应该考究各朝各代的世系，明白其盛衰的原因，只有这样才能从历史中汲取教训。

136

After finishing these,
Read histories please.
Do study genealogy,
And know causality.

After you have finished the classic and sophistic books,
you can read annals. When you do this,
you should inquire into the genealogies of the dynasties,
learn the causes of the vicissitudes, and draw lessons from them.

137

学

Learning

History

自羲农，
至黄帝。
号三皇，
居上世。

伏羲氏、神农氏和黄帝是三位上古时代的先驱，他们勤政爱民，开拓有功，被后人尊称为『三皇』。

The legendary Fooshee, Shennong and Huangdee
Were great forefathers, Esteemed Three Rulers.

Fooshee, Shennong and Huangdee,
the forefathers who pioneered the land and
took care of the masses,
were esteemed Three Emperors.

Yao and You-yuh, Called Grandees Two.
They demised throne, A heyday known.

After Huangdee came two greatest figures
of all times, Yao and Shun.
Yao, unsatisfied with his son,
demised his throne to the able Shun.
Under their governance,
there appeared a heyday in China.

黄帝之后，还有两位贤明的帝王，叫唐尧和虞舜。尧认为儿子不肖，便把帝位传给了贤能的舜。两位帝王开创了华夏的人间盛世。

唐有虞，号二帝。相揖逊，称盛世。

Hsiah, Shang, Chough, Three dynasties, lo.
Yuh, Tang, Wuh, Three kings true.

Yuh founded Hsiah, Tang founded Shang, and Wuh founded Chough.
These three figures were called Three Kings because of their great merits.

夏有禹，商有汤，周文武，称三王。

夏朝的开国君主是禹，商朝的开国君主是汤，周朝的开国君主是武王。这几位君主德才兼备，被后人尊称为『三王』。

夏传子，
家天下。
四百载，
迁夏社。

大禹把帝位传给了自己的儿子，开启了君王的世袭制。
四百多年之后，夏被汤所灭。

Yuh, heredity begun, Throned his son.
Four centuries passed, Seeing Hsiah's last.

Yuh passed his throne on to his son,
hence the hereditary system of the crown.
More than four hundred years later,
Hsiah was annulled by Tang.

145

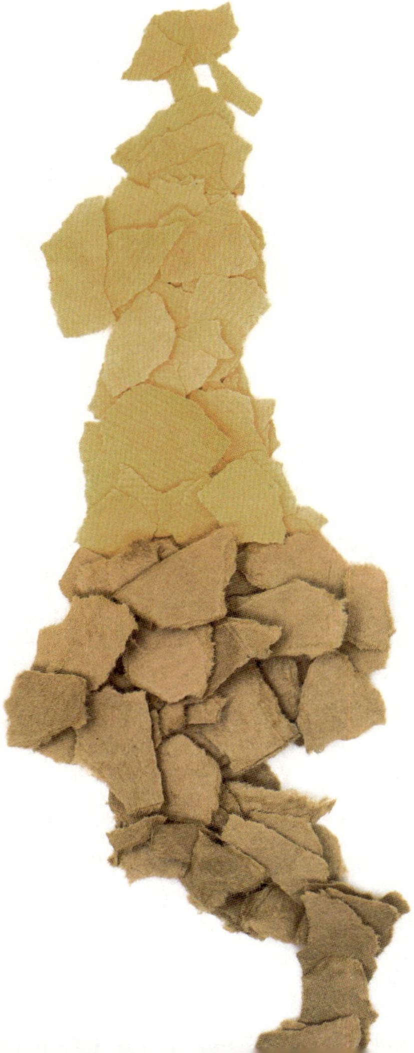

The Conqueror Tang Founded Kingdom Shang.
Six centuries' elapse Ere Chow's collapse.

King Tang finished Hsiah
and founded the Shang Dynasty,
which lasted six hundred years
before its end at Chow's Era.

汤伐夏，国号商。六百载，至纣亡。

商汤王起兵灭掉了夏，建立了商朝。商朝前后延续约六百年，至商纣王时灭亡。

Wuh of Chough Triumphed over Chow. Eight centuries' gain, Chough's longest reign.

Wuh founded the Chough Dynasty
after having nullified the Shang Dynasty
and killed Chow the tyrant.
Chough lasted more than eight hundred years,
the longest of all dynasties
in the Chinese history.

周武王，始诛纣。八百载，最长久。

周武王杀死商纣王，灭掉商朝，建立了周朝。周朝在中国所有朝代中历史最长，前后延续了八百多年。

周辙东，王纲坠。逞干戈，尚游说。

自从周朝东迁国都之后，便很难有效地管理诸侯了。诸侯国之间战争不断，而游说之士也开始大行其道。

Chough moved east, And controlled least.
There arose militance; Valued was eloquence.

Chough moved its capital east,
hence the Eastern Chough.
The Chough House had less and
less control over its vassals.
There were often wars among the vassal states,
and lobbyists held sway.

Spring 'n Fall began, Warring States then.
Five Lords strived! Seven Powers thrived!

The Eastern Chough
was divided into two periods,
the Spring 'n Fall period
and the Warring States period.
Huan of Chih, Xiang of Song,
Wen of Jin, Muh of Chin, and Tsuang
of Chuh became predominant,
called Five Lords. The seven powers
in the Warring States period were
the State of Chih, the State of Chuh,
the State of Yan, the State of Han,
the State of Weigh,
and the State of Chin.

东周分为前后两个阶段，前期史称春秋，后期为战国。春秋时期有著名的五霸，为齐桓公、宋襄公、晋文公、秦穆公和楚庄王。战国时七个诸侯国很强大，称为七雄，分别是齐楚燕韩赵魏秦。

始春秋，
终战国。
五霸强，
七雄出。

Emperor the First, Other states burst.
Generations but two, Arose Han'n Chuh.

At the end of the Warring States period,
the State of Chin became more and
more powerful. Under the king
who termed himself as Emperor the First,
Chin annexed other six powers,
and founded the unitary Chin Dynasty.
At the second reign of the dynasty,
the country was thrown into a turmoil,
hence the contention
between Chuh and Han.

嬴秦氏，始兼并。传二世，楚汉争。

战国末年，秦国崛起，日渐强大。秦王嬴政兼并六国，建立了统一的秦朝，自称始皇帝。秦传到二世，天下又开始大乱，最后形成楚汉相争的局面。

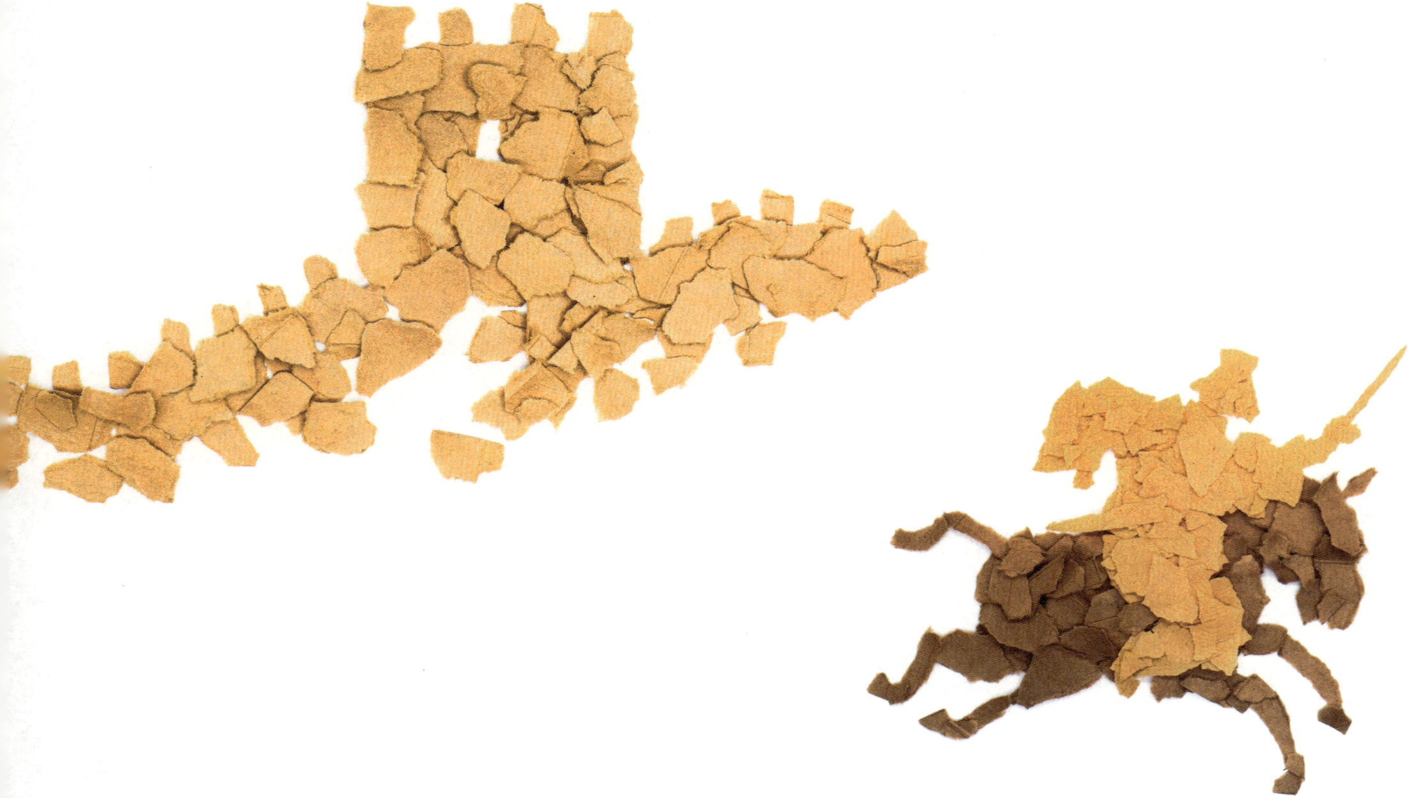

高祖兴，
汉业建。
至孝平，
王莽篡。

汉高祖刘邦在楚汉相争中获胜，建立了汉朝。汉朝历时两百余年，到了孝平皇帝时，被王莽篡了位。

Liu Bang almighty ran; Arose Great Han.
Hsiao Ping was bayed; So Wang Mang swayed.

The Han Dynasty arose with Liu Bang's victory over his opponent. This dynasty lasted more than two hundred years until Wang Mang usurped the throne of Emperor Hsiao Ping.

光武兴，为东汉。四百年，终于献。

王莽篡权，导致天下大乱。刘秀推翻更始帝，恢复国号为汉，史称东汉光武帝。汉朝延续四百年，到汉献帝时灭亡。

With Guang Wuh began The Eastern Han.
Th' four hundredth year, Hanhsian died drear.

Wang Mang's usurpation threw the world into upheavals. Liu Hsiu, i.e. Emperor Guang Wuh, overthrew Emperor Gengshih and restored the Han Dynasty, hence the Eastern Han. The Han Dynasty lasted four hundred years until Emperor Hanhsian died.

Shuh, Woo, Weigh Struggled their way,
Three kingdoms reared; Two Jins appeared.

In the last years of
the Eastern Han Dynasty,
Weigh, Shuh, and Woo fought against
each other, hence the
Three Kingdom period. At last,
Weigh annulled Shuh and Woo,
but it was soon superseded by
the Jin Dynasty when Sihma Yan
usurped the throne.
Jin includes two periods,
the Western Jin and the Eastern Jin.

魏蜀吴，争汉鼎。号三国，迄两晋。

东汉末年，魏国、蜀国、吴国争夺天下，形成三国相争的局面。后来魏灭了蜀国和吴国，但又被司马炎篡夺了帝位，建立了晋朝，晋又分为东晋和西晋两个时期。

Song, Chih, Liang, And Chen sprang.
Each Southern king, Seated in Nanking.

Soon after it moved south,
the Jin House died out.
Then came the Southern and
Northern Dynasties period.
The Southern Dynasties include Song,
Chih, Liang, and Chen,
all seated in Nanking.

宋齐继，梁陈承。
为南朝，都金陵。

晋朝王室南迁之后，不久就衰亡了，继之而起的是南北朝时代。南朝包括宋齐梁陈，国都都建在南京。

Northern Weigh, pressed, Divided, east 'n west.
Yuhwen founded Chough, Chih followed though.

The Northern Courts started from
the Northern Weigh,
which later was divided into the Eastern Weigh
and the Western Weigh.
The Eastern Weigh was usurped
by Yuhwen, who established
the Northern Chough,
and the Western Weigh
was usurped by Gao Yang,
who established the Northern Chih.

北朝始自北魏，北魏也叫元魏。北魏后来又分裂成东魏和西魏。西魏被宇文觉篡了位，建立了北周；东魏被高洋篡了位，建立了北齐。

北元魏，
分东西。
宇文周，
兴高齐。

Suih, so grand, United the land.
It did bloom Before its doom.

Yang Jian established the Suih Dynasty,
and China was united again.
Before soon it was superseded
by the Tang Dynasty,
due to the debauchery of Emperor Suih Yang,
who was Yang Jian's son.

迨至隋，一土宇。不再传，失统绪。

杨坚重新统一中国，建立了隋朝。他的儿子隋炀帝杨广即位。由于他荒淫无道，隋朝很快就灭亡了。

Li Yuan's uprising now Swept Suih enow.
Th'Tang Empire rose At Suih's close.

Li Yuan raised troops against Suih,
defeated many opponents,
and set up the Tang Dynasty as Suih was finished.

唐高祖，起义师。除隋乱，创国基。

唐高祖李渊起兵反隋，他战胜了各路反隋义军，夺取天下，建立了唐朝。

二十传，
三百载。
梁灭之，
国乃改。

唐朝的统治近三百年，总共传了二十位皇帝。唐哀帝被朱全忠篡位，梁朝建立了，唐朝从此灭亡。为了和南北朝时期的梁相区别，历史上称为后梁。

Three century's gains Made twenty reigns.
There arose Liang That replaced Tang.

The Tang Dynasty reigned for nearly three hundred years, with twenty emperors in all. Emperor Tang-Ai was usurped by Chu Quanchong, who founded the Liang Dynasty, termed the Latter Liang to be distinguished from the former Liang.

梁唐晋，及汉周。称五代，皆有由。

后梁之后或在此期间，还有后唐、后晋、后汉和后周。这段时间历史上称作『五代』。

Thus started Liang, Jin and Tang,
Han and Chough; Five you know.

After, and concurrent with,
the Latter Liang,
there were the Latter Tang,
the Latter Jin, the Latter Han,
and the Latter Chough,
and this period is called the Five Dynasties.

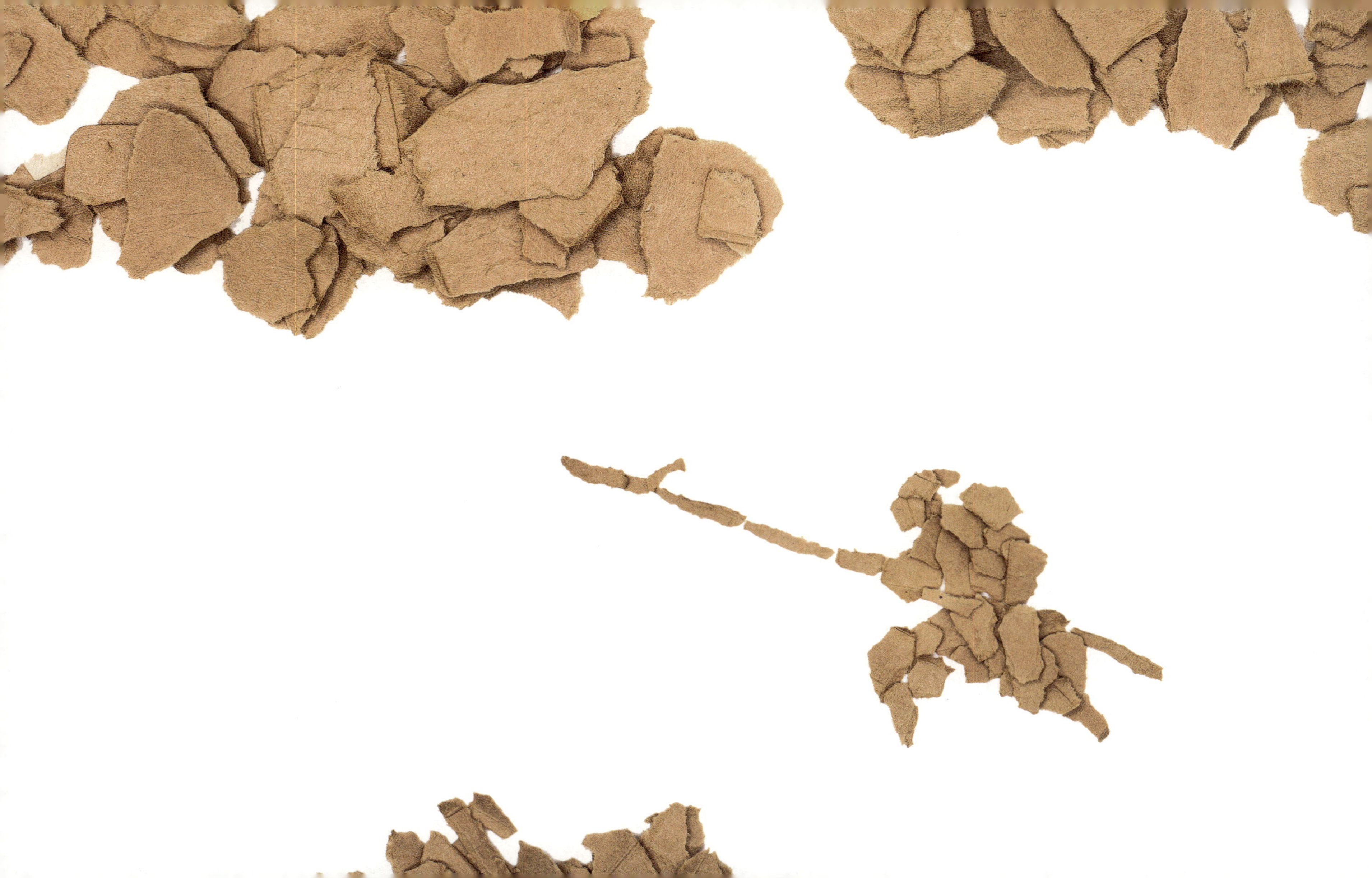

Then Song, aglow, Succeeded to Chough.
Reigns counted eighteen, Then invasions keen.

Chao Kuangyin,
accepting the demised throne of
the Latter Chough,
founded the Song Dynasty.
At the eighteenth emperor's reign,
the ethnics from the north invaded the land,
hence scuffles between
the north and the south.

炎宋兴，
受周禅。
十八传，
南北混。

赵匡胤接受了后周『禅让』的帝位，建立了宋朝。宋朝传了十八位皇帝之后，北方的少数民族南下侵扰，结果又成了南北混战的局面。

Liao and Jin Both broke in.
The Mongol throng Wiped out Song.

Liao, Jin, and Mongols in
the north established their polities and
their chieftains claimed to be emperors.
In the end, the Mongols annulled Jin and
Song and set up the Yuan Dynasty,
hence the reunification of China.

辽与金，
皆称帝。
元灭金，
绝宋世。

北方的辽人、金人和蒙古人都建立了国家，都自称皇帝。最后，蒙古人灭了金朝和宋朝，建立了元朝，再一次统一了中国。

舆图广，超前代。九十年，国祚废。

元朝疆域辽阔，其领土超过了以前的任何一个朝代。然而，它只维持了短短的九十年，就被农民起义推翻了。

The territory vast Exceeded all past. Ninety years elapsed; The empire collapsed.

The Yuan Dynasty had a territory larger than any other previous dynasties. However, it lasted only ninety years before it was overthrown by a peasant uprising.

Eighth by name Won his fame.
By founding Ming, Seated in Nanking

At the end of the Yuan Dynasty,
Chu Yuanchang's peasant uprising overthrew
the reign of the Mongolian Empire.
Chu Yuanchang founded the Ming Dynasty,
coronated himself as its first emperor,
hence Taitsuh (the beginning father).
And the Ming's capital was Nanking.

元朝末年，明太祖朱元璋起义，最后推翻了元朝的统治，建立了大明，国号洪武。他登基当上了皇帝，定都在金陵。

太祖兴，
国大明。
号洪武，
都金陵。

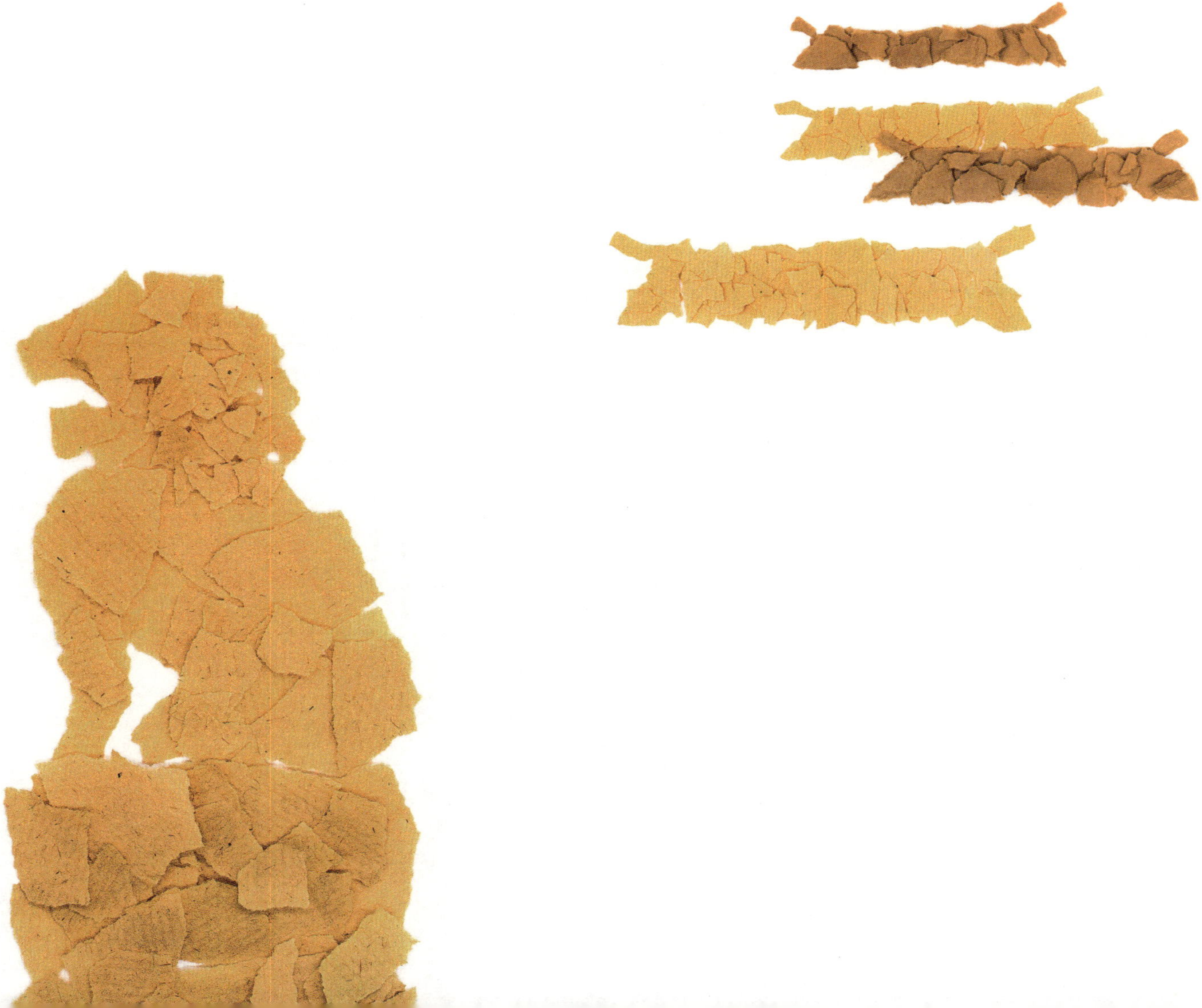

迨成祖，迁燕京。
十六世，至崇祯。

到明成祖即位后，便把国都由金陵迁到燕京。明朝共传了十六个皇帝，直到崇祯皇帝为止，明朝就灭亡了。

Chengtsuh from Nanking Moved to Peking.
Sixteen emperors past, Chongchen the last.

After his coronation,
Chengtsuh moved the capital from
Nanking to Peking.
There were sixteen emperors
in the Ming Dynasty,
Chongchen being the last.

The eunuch power Made all cower.
King of Spurt Did Ming subvert.

In the last years of the Ming Dynasty, eunuch officials abused their power to such an extent that there were uprisings in many places.
Li Chicheng, the so-called King of Spurt, broke into Peking (Beijing) and subverted the Ming Dynasty.

阉祸后，寇内讧。闯逆变，神器终。

明朝末年，宦官专权，天下大乱，老百姓纷纷起义。以闯王李自成为首的起义军攻破北京，明朝最后灭亡。

Diligence

动

以上所叙述的是从三皇五帝直到今天的历史。从中大家可以了解各朝各代的治乱兴衰，学会很多有用的东西。

What has been talked above is the history
from antiquity up to now,
from which one can learn lessons
from the rise and fall of all the dynasties.

古今史，全在兹。载治乱，知兴衰。

History is here, Until this year. You know all: Rise and fall.

史虽繁，读有次。史记一，汉书二。

中国历史浩繁复杂，读史书者应当讲究方法，循序渐进，先读史记，再读汉书。

Since Chinese history is so complicated,
you should read it in good order,
History Book first, then *Han Annals*.

Read history vast, First to last. *History Book* begun, *Han Annals* anon.

勤

Diligence

第三读后汉书，第四读三国志，读这些史书的同时，还要参照经书，参考资治通鉴。这样，我们就可以更好地了解历史的治乱兴衰了。

You can proceed to read *Eastern Han* and *Three Kingdoms*.
While you study these authorized books,
you can consult the classics and
Mirrors so that you can have a better idea
of what happened in Chinese history.

后汉三，国志四。兼证经，参通鉴。

Next *Eastern Han*, *Three Kingdoms* then. Consult the authorized With *Mirrors* beside.

读史者，考实录。通古今，若亲目。

读历史的人应该更进一步地去翻阅历史资料，了解古往今来的前因后果，就好像是自己亲眼所见一样。

Those who are interested in history
can check historical records to go through the incidents
as if they see them happen themselves.

As past's explored, Check every record. You'll know how Then became now.

口而诵，

心而惟。

朝于斯，

夕于斯。

Read and think, And pieces link. From early morning, To late evening.

大家读书时，应该放声朗诵，同时还要用心去思考。只有早晚都把心思用到学习上，才能真正学好。

When you do your reading, you should read aloud and contemplate. Only when you are devoted to learning can you learn well.

189

勤

Diligence

从前，孔子是个十分好学的人。当时鲁国有一位神童名叫项橐，孔子就曾向他学习。像孔子这样伟大的圣贤，尚不忘勤学，何况我们普通人呢？

Confucius was a good learner.
Once he met a prodigy called Hsiang Tuo
in the Luh State and consulted him.
Even a sage like Confucius was so intent on his studies,
shouldn't we follow his example?

昔仲尼，师项橐。古圣贤，尚勤学。

Confucius of yore, Studied, studied more. From Tuo learned, As he yearned.

宋朝宰相赵普，尽管身居要职，天天还手不释卷地阅读《论语》。

Chao Puh, the famous premier of the Song Dynasty, studied the *Analects* intensively everyday, although he was in such a high position.

赵中令，读鲁论。彼既仕，学且勤。

Chao Puh of Song, Read *Analects* long. This premier crack, Was never slack.

西汉时，路温舒把文字抄在蒲草上阅读，而公孙弘则将春秋刻在竹子削成的竹片上。他们两人都很穷，买不起书，但还不忘勤奋学习。

In the Western Han Dynasty,
Lu Wenshoo copied words on cattail tips for reading,
and Gongsun Hong carved *Spring 'n Fall* on bamboo slips.
They, both poor, couldn't afford to buy books,
but they pressed on to study.

披蒲编，
削竹简。
彼无书，
且知勉。

Using cattail tips, And bamboo slips. None they possessed, Persisting with zest.

晋朝时的孙敬和战国时的苏秦发奋读书，穷而愈坚，悲而能壮。为了不犯困，一个把头发悬挂在屋梁上，一个用锥子刺自己的大腿。

Sun Jing in the Jin Dynasty and
Soo Qin in the Warring States period were poverty-stricken.
However, they were so determined as to be serious with their study. One kept his hair hung from a beam,
another needled his thigh lest they should feel sleepy.

头悬梁，锥刺股。彼不教，自勤苦。

Head strung high! Needled his thigh! Not pushed, they Kept working away.

勤

Diligence

196

晋朝时车胤读书时把萤火虫放在纱袋里采光照明，还有一位叫孙康的则以雪的反光来看书。他们的生活条件如此艰苦却能持之以恒地读书。

To carry on with their reading,
Che Yin in the Jin Dynasty
kept fireworms in a gauze bag to produce light,
and Sun Kang made use of the reflection from snow.
They could manage to study
even in such unfavorable conditions.

如囊萤，
如映雪。
家虽贫，
学不辍。

With fireworms bright, With snow white. Poor, having none, They studied on.

汉朝的朱买臣，以砍柴为生，往往一边担柴一边读书。隋朝的李密把书挂在牛角上，一有时间就读。

Chuh Maichen in the Han Dynasty
chopped firewood for a living.
He kept reading while carrying firewood on his back.
And Li Mih hung his book on a horn of his cow
and made time to read it.

如负薪，
如挂角。
身虽劳，
犹苦卓。

Carrying fuel now, Book on cow, They, making time, Employed their prime.

勤

Diligence

苏老泉，
二十七。
始发愤，
读书籍。

Twenty seven, Quan Hadn't studied then. This man now Read hard enow.

宋朝的苏老泉，即苏洵，二十七岁时才立志读书，发奋图强而成为学问大家，名列唐宋八大家。

Suh Laoquan, i.e. ,Suh Hsun, didn't make his mind to study
until he was twenty seven.
He finally succeeded as a famous scholar,
enjoying the prestige as one of the eight greatest men of letters
in the Tang and the Song Dynasties.

彼既老，
犹悔迟。
尔小生，
宜早思。

苏老泉成年之后才认识到读书的重要性。我们年轻人难道不应该抓紧时间好好学习吗？

Only when he was a grown-up
did he realize the importance of learning.
Don't we need to make use of our time to study
while we are young?

This man, behold, Started when old. You'd make time Even ere prime.

宋朝时期有个叫梁灏的，他在八十二岁时才考中状元，在金銮殿上对皇帝的提问能够对答如流，其他生员皆不如他。

There was a man called Liang Hao in the Song Dynasty,
who passed Grand Test
(the Imperial Examination) at the age of 82.
He defended himself so well when the emperor questioned him
at the court that he was better than
all other examinees.

若梁灏，八十二。对大廷，魁多士。

Liang, Wizard True, At eighty two, Passed Grand Test, Beating the rest.

彼既成，众称异。尔小生，宜立志。

His great success Did all impress. While you're young, Make wills strong.

梁灏如此高龄，尚能获得成功，让众人感到诧异。大家趁着年轻，难道不该立志向学吗？

Liang Hao succeeded at such an advanced age, surprising everybody. Shouldn't we make up our mind to learn while we are young?

北齐有个叫祖莹的人八岁就能写诗，

唐朝的李泌七岁就能以象棋为题赋诗。

Chuh Ying in the North Qih Dynasty
could compose poems at eight,
and Li Mih in the Tang Dynasty
could even rhyme chess playing at seven.

莹八岁，能咏诗。

泌七岁，能赋棋。

Ying, so great, Versified at eight. Mih rhymed even Then at seven.

彼颖悟，人称奇。尔幼学，当效之。

他们两人的聪明才智让世人羡慕，称奇。我们也当效法他们，及早地努力学习。

They were admired for their talents and performance.
We should follow suit and start as early as possible.

They, so clever, Praised with wonder. Like them, begin Now to win.

中国古代还有一些出色的女才子，比如东汉末年的蔡文姬能听出琴声的好坏，晋朝的谢道韫则能出口成章，即兴作诗。

And there were some talented girls in ancient China,
for example, Cai Wenjih
could discern the quality of a zithern by the ear,
and Hsieh Daoyun managed
to compose a poem at short notice.

蔡文姬，能辨琴。谢道韫，能咏吟。

Cai could discern An ill-tuned zithern. Hsieh could prose, Or poems compose.

这些女孩子都如此聪慧多才，身为好男儿更应当自强。

Girls like them could be so accomplished;
as men you should sustain yourselves.

彼女子，且聪敏。尔男子，当自警。

These girls above Did smart prove. Man thou art, Devote thy heart!

唐刘晏，
方七岁。
举神童，
作正字。

唐玄宗时，有一个小孩子名叫刘晏，当时才只有七岁，就被推举为神童，并且做了负责刊正文字的官。

In the reign of Tang Hsuantsong,
a seven-year-old boy named Liu Yan was promoted to be an imperial proofreader.

Now Yan, behold, Seven years old. Proofread did he, Such a prodigy.

彼虽幼，
身已仕。
有为者，
亦若是。

刘晏年纪这么小就做了官，担当国家给他的重任。大家只要勤奋好学，也可以和刘晏一样名扬后世。

Young as Liu Yan was,
he was given an important position.
If one works hard,
he can be as successful as Liu Yan.

Young as he, An official already. To be well-done, Follow this one.

犬守夜，鸡司晨。苟不学，曷为人。

狗在夜间守护家门；鸡在天亮时报晓。人如果不能用心学习而糟蹋时光，那么还有什么资格称为人呢？

Dogs keep the door at night,
and cocks crow to tell good morning.
If one loafs around,
doing nothing,
how can he be called man?

Dogs thieves bite; Cocks dawning invite. Unless you learn, Useless you'll turn.

蚕吐丝，

蜂酿蜜。

人不学，

不如物。

蚕吐丝以供我们做衣料；蜜蜂酿蜜以供我们食用。人如果不懂得学习，以自己的知识和技能来服务社会，那还不如小动物呢。

Silkworms provide us with silk,
and bees provide us with honey.
If one does not acquire knowledge to serve the society,
he is not as worthwhile as such small things.

Silkworms silk educe; Bees honey produce. From them learn, Or receive spurn.

217

勤

Diligence

幼而学，
壮而行。
上致君，
下泽民。

从幼年开始，我们就应当努力学习，积累知识。只有这样，我们长大后才能够学以致用，替国家效力，为人民谋福利。

We should start early to learn and improve ourselves so that when we grow up we can serve the country and the people.

Learn while young; Act while strong. Benefit each one Under the sun.

218

扬名声，显父母。光于前，裕于后。

如果你能有所作为，有益于社会，人民就会颂扬你，父母也会感到荣耀。你给祖先增添了光彩，也给后代树立了好的榜样。

If you have done your bit for the society,
you will be remembered for that,
and your parents and even ancestors will share your glory,
and your descendants can follow your example.

Carve your name And parents' fame. Ancestors you glorify; Offspring you dignify.

人遗子，金满籝。我教子，唯一经。

For children hold Silver and gold? My only bequest: Learn your best.

很多人给子孙后代积攒钱财，而我并不这样。我留给他们的遗产只是教诲：希望他们能够读书学习，好好做人。

Many people save money for their children.
But I don't do this.
My bequest for them is the teaching, that is,
they should try their best to learn.

222

勤有功，戏无益。戒之哉，宜勉力。

No pains, no gains.
If one squanders time,
he will regret later on.
You should guard against laziness,
and go ahead with fortitude.

凡是勤奋上进的人，都会有好的收获，而如果某人只顾贪玩，浪费了大好时光，最后一定会后悔的。因此，大家应当戒除懒惰的诱惑，勉力向前。

Good is diligence; Poor is negligence. Trials you breast, Work with zest.

223

勤

Diligence

跋

Afterword

2011年8月11日午休时间，躺在天外招待所的榻榻米上，突发奇想：三字经如果英译，那么『三字』这一凸显特征该如何表现呢？能否以三个英语单词对应汉语的三个字来译呢？起身欲试，马上便译出第一节，而且用了偶韵，于是拟定三词格偶韵体的格局，准备将英韵三字经嵌入这预制的模板。本打算一个月之内完成译稿，可是竟停不下来，只好往下译。两天半，译完了！左眼有点朦胧——电脑前坐久了；右手臂有点痛——鼠标动多了。尽管如此，心中却充溢着翻译之乐。两天前的奇想竟然变为现实了！且不论拙译能否与原著比肩，但是仅就诗体形式而言，这至少是名副其实的英韵三字经了。各路译家无论多么卓绝不凡，如果没有再现『三字』，如何敢称自己的译作是三字经？在随后的几天里，慢慢享受着修改的乐趣。

不知道世界上是否有人以三个英语单词对应三字经的三个汉字来翻译此部小小的巨著，而且还是韵文乃至偶韵的译作。如果有，那么两个版本相对比必是神奇无比——在严格的限制之内竟有两个版本上演语言的杂技；如果没有，我想此译便是富有积极意义的尝试了。它欲以戴着脚镣跳舞的风姿来演绎翻译的神奇。在以异国语言展示中华魅力的同时，它可以给韵文翻译提供一个样例，也可以启示译之为易的翻译原理。

我准备出版一本英韵三字经。为了便于老外理解，我花了好多天的时间给文本加上中英文的白话解释。这可以作为辅助性的阅读材料。当然，读者完全可以不理睬这些内容，因为三字经的译语文本是自主、自足的。这是英文版的国学经典。

为了验证英韵三字经（*Three Word Primer*）的可读性，我对美国的母子二人进行了阅读测试。儿子只有15岁，我担心他可能看不懂。没想到他不仅句句都懂还兴致很高，满脸笑容，连

连竖起大拇指。随后，他母亲也通读了文本。她对这简短的文字感到十分惊奇，连说『like proverbs』。就『Son of Man』这一用法，她还想证实我是否知道它的典故。看来，这母子二人阅读上毫无障碍，而且还能欣赏。这不正是我预期中的效果吗？

文字是神奇的！英汉两种语言可谓是天壤之别，而译者竟能窥视上帝调变语言的天机，用一种文字精细地传达另一种文字，并使之成为形神兼备的艺术品。你不得不赞叹造物主的伟大——他分化了语言也造就了译者！

三字经是神圣的！这部被誉为『袖里通鉴纲目』的千古奇书已经融进中华民族的血液，切切实实成了她的文化基因。

要用这文字的神奇再铸三字经这一神圣的经典，却是对译者最严酷的考验，因为语言是上帝设置的密码，而个体语言之间有一道很难逾越的天堑，加之三字经是中华元素最密集、文字最凝练的韵文，译者更难跨越。西方传教士也早有断言：三字经『不能译为英文韵诗』〔H. A. Giles, Autobibliographical, etc., Add. MS. 8964 (1). Cambridge University Library, p.14.〕。译者如果不能借助神力而力有不逮或者缺少神圣的使命感，便很有可能摔入谷底——勉强成文的译语『经典』便是跌入谷底之作，自然没有原典的超拔与光彩。

吕叔湘曾如此论翻译：稍一不慎，流弊丛生。惟其如此，佳译难得一见，何况是以诗译诗，更何况是三字经这电报体的三词格偶韵体的韵文。于是，我不断对比原作与译稿，联系历史语境，字斟句酌，以便随时修改，以使译文更靠近原文，使之更具有原典性和文学性，乃至逼近原文的语体和风格。比如，在译苏老泉『始发愤，读书籍』时，我先是以『Now this lad/Read like mad』对译，真是感到惬意，甚至觉得它堪当形意俱佳的典

范，但反思之后觉得有点口语化，与三字经典雅的风格有所不合，所以重新措辞，改为『This man now/Read hard enow』。为了使译文更加精炼，有的地方置换了译文，比如『幼不学，老何为』，最初译为『A poor-learning youth, /Will turn uncouth.』。诗行略显参差，措辞略感生涩，故而改为名词结构且各成分彼此对称的『A young loafer,/An old loser.』，真可谓笔曲而达。

经典不容懈怠！哪怕改善一词，都让人兴奋不已。斟酌至此，想必还有许多不理想之处。希望这部英译三字经能像酿酒一样不断地提纯。

为了经典，我们期待更像经典的译作。

赵彦春　2016 年 5 月

三字经全文
（汉语拼音版）

Three Word Primer (Pinyin Version)

jiào

教

rén zhī chū
人之初，
xìng běn shàn
性本善。
xìng xiāng jìn
性相近，
xí xiāng yuǎn
习相远。

gǒu bù jiào
苟不教，
xìng nǎi qiān
性乃迁。
jiào zhī dào
教之道，
guì yǐ zhuān
贵以专。

xī mèng mǔ
昔孟母，
zé lín chǔ
择邻处，
zǐ bù xué
子不学，
duàn jī zhù
断机杼。

dòu yàn shān
窦燕山，
yǒu yì fāng
有义方，
jiào wǔ zǐ
教五子，
míng jù yáng
名俱扬。

yǎng bù jiào
养不教，
fù zhī guò
父之过。
jiào bù yán
教不严，
shī zhī duò
师之惰。

zǐ bù xué
子不学，
fēi suǒ yí
非所宜。
yòu bù xué
幼不学，
lǎo hé wéi
老何为？

yù bù zhuó
玉不琢，
bù chéng qì
不成器。
rén bù xué
人不学，
bù zhī yì
不知义。

wéi rén zǐ
为人子，
fāng shào shí
方少时，
qīn shī yǒu
亲师友，
xí lǐ yí
习礼仪。

xiāng jiǔ líng
香九龄，
néng wēn xí
能温席。
xiào yú qīn
孝于亲，
suǒ dāng zhí
所当执。

róng sì suì
融四岁，
néng ràng lí
能让梨。
tì yú cháng
弟于长，
yí xiān zhī
宜先知。

shǒu xiào tì
首孝悌，
cì jiàn wén
次见闻，
zhī mǒu shù
知某数，
shí mǒu wén
识某文。

zhī
知

yī ér shí
一而十，
shí ér bǎi
十而百，
bǎi ér qiān
百而千，
qiān ér wàn
千而万。

sān cái zhě
三才者，
tiān dì rén
天地人。
sān guāng zhě
三光者，
rì yuè xīng
日月星。

sān gāng zhě
三纲者，
jūn chén yì
君臣义。
fù zǐ qīn
父子亲，
fū fù shùn
夫妇顺。

yuē chūn xià
曰春夏，
yuē qiū dōng
曰秋冬，
cǐ sì shí
此四时，
yùn bù qióng
运不穷。

yuē nán běi
曰南北，
yuē xī dōng
曰西东，
cǐ sì fāng
此四方，
yìng hū zhōng
应乎中。

yuē shuǐ huǒ
曰水火，
mù jīn tǔ
木金土，
cǐ wǔ xíng
此五行，
běn hū shù
本乎数。

shí gān zhě
十干者，
jiǎ zhì guǐ
甲至癸。
shí èr zhī
十二支，
zǐ zhì hài
子至亥。

yuē huáng dào
曰黄道，
rì suǒ chán
日所躔。
yuē chì dào
曰赤道，
dāng zhōng quán
当中权。

chì dào xià
赤道下，
wēn nuǎn jí
温暖极。
wǒ zhōng huá
我中华，
zài dōng běi
在东北。

hán yù jūn
寒燠均，
shuāng lù gǎi
霜露改。
yòu gāo yuán
右高原，
zuǒ dà hǎi
左大海。

yuē jiāng hé
曰江河，
yuē huái jì
曰淮济。
cǐ sì dú
此四渎，
shuǐ zhī jì
水之纪。

yuē dài huá
曰岱华，
sōng héng héng
嵩恒衡。
cǐ wǔ yuè
此五岳，
shān zhī míng
山之名。

yuē shì nóng
曰士农，
yuē gōng shāng
曰工商。
cǐ sì mín
此四民，
guó zhī liáng
国之良。

yuē rén yì
曰仁义，
lǐ zhì xìn
礼智信，
cǐ wǔ cháng
此五常，
bù róng wěn
不容紊。

dì suǒ shēng
地所生，
yǒu cǎo mù
有草木。
cǐ zhí wù
此植物，
biàn shuǐ lù
遍水陆。

yǒu chóng yú
有虫鱼，
yǒu niǎo shòu
有鸟兽。
cǐ dòng wù
此动物，
néng fēi zǒu
能飞走。

dào liáng shū
稻粱菽，
mài shǔ jì
麦黍稷，
cǐ liù gǔ
此六谷，
rén suǒ shí
人所食。

mǎ niú yáng
马牛羊，
jī quǎn shǐ
鸡犬豕，
cǐ liù xù
此六畜，
rén suǒ sì
人所饲。

yuē xǐ nù
曰喜怒，
yuē āi jù
曰哀惧，
ài wù yù
爱恶欲，
qī qíng jù
七情具。

qīng chì huáng
青赤黄，
jí hēi bái
及黑白。
cǐ wǔ sè
此五色，
mù suǒ shí
目所识。

suān kǔ gān
酸苦甘，
jí xīn xián
及辛咸。
cǐ wǔ wèi
此五味，
kǒu suǒ hán
口所含。

shān jiāo xiāng
膻焦香，
jí xīng xiǔ
及腥朽。
cǐ wǔ xiù
此五臭，
bí suǒ xiù
鼻所嗅。

páo tǔ gé
匏土革，
mù shí jīn
木石金，
sī yǔ zhú
丝与竹，
nǎi bā yīn
乃八音。

yuē píng shǎng
曰平上，
yuē qù rù
曰去入。
cǐ sì shēng
此四声，
yí tiáo xié
宜调协。

gāo zēng zǔ
高曾祖，
fù ér shēn
父而身，
shēn ér zǐ
身而子，
zǐ ér sūn
子而孙。

zì zǐ sūn
自子孙，
zhì xuán zēng
至玄曾，
nǎi jiǔ zú
乃九族，
rén zhī lún
人之伦。

fù zǐ ēn
父子恩，
fū fù cóng
夫妇从。
xiōng zé yǒu
兄则友，
dì zé gōng
弟则恭。

zhǎng yòu xù
长幼序，
yǒu yǔ péng
友与朋。
jūn zé jìng
君则敬，
chén zé zhōng
臣则忠。

cǐ shí yì
此十义，
rén suǒ tóng
人所同。
dāng shī xù
当师叙，
wù wéi bèi
勿违背。

zhǎn qí shuāi
斩齐衰，
dà xiǎo gōng
大小功。
zhì sī má
至缌麻，
wǔ fú zhōng
五服终。

yǒu gǔ wén
有古文，
dà xiǎo zhuàn
大小篆。
lì cǎo jì
隶草继，
bù kě luàn
不可乱。

xué
学

ruò guǎng xué，jù qí fán。dàn lüè shuō，néng zhī yuán。
若广学，惧其繁。但略说，能知原。

lǐ yuè shè，yù shū shù。gǔ liù yì，jīn bù jù。
礼乐射，御书数。古六艺，今不具。

wéi shū xué，rén gòng zūn。jì shí zì，jiǎng shuō wén。
惟书学，人共遵。既识字，讲说文。

fán xùn méng，xū jiǎng jiū，xiáng xùn gǔ，míng jù dòu。
凡训蒙，须讲究，详训诂，明句读。

wéi xué zhě，bì yǒu chū，xiǎo xué zhōng，zhì sì shū。
为学者，必有初，小学终，至四书。

lùn yǔ zhě，èr shí piān，qún dì zǐ，jì shàn yán。
论语者，二十篇，群弟子，记善言。

mèng zǐ zhě，qī piān zhǐ，jiǎng dào dé，shuō rén yì。
孟子者，七篇止，讲道德，说仁义。

zuò zhōng yōng，nǎi kǒng jí，zhōng bù piān，yōng bù yì。
作中庸，乃孔伋，中不偏，庸不易。

zuò dà xué，nǎi zēng zǐ，zì xiū qí，zhì píng zhì。
作大学，乃曾子，自修齐，至平治。

xiào jīng tōng
孝经通，
sì shū shú
四书熟，
rú liù jīng
如六经，
shǐ kě dú
始可读。

shī shū yì
诗书易，
lǐ chūn qiū
礼春秋，
hào liù jīng
号六经，
dāng jiǎng qiú
当讲求。

yǒu lián shān
有连山，
yǒu guī cáng
有归藏，
yǒu zhōu yì
有周易，
sān yì xiáng
三易详。

yǒu diǎn mó
有典谟，
yǒu xùn gào
有训诰，
yǒu shì mìng
有誓命，
shū zhī ào
书之奥。

wǒ zhōu gōng
我周公，
zuò zhōu lǐ
作周礼，
zhù liù guān
著六官，
cún zhì tǐ
存治体。

dà xiǎo dài
大小戴，
zhù lǐ jì
注礼记，
shù shèng yán
述圣言，
lǐ yuè bèi
礼乐备。

yuē guó fēng
曰国风，
yuē yǎ sòng
曰雅颂，
hào sì shī
号四诗，
dāng fěng yǒng
当讽咏。

shī jì wáng
诗既亡，
chūn qiū zuò
春秋作，
yù bāo biǎn
寓褒贬，
bié shàn è
别善恶。

sān zhuàn zhě
三传者，
yǒu gōng yáng
有公羊，
yǒu zuǒ shì
有左氏，
yǒu gǔ liáng
有谷梁。

jīng jì míng
经既明，
fāng dú zǐ
方读子，
cuō qí yào
撮其要，
jì qí shì
记其事。

wǔ zǐ zhě
五子者，
yǒu xún yáng
有荀扬。
wén zhōng zǐ
文中子，
jí lǎo zhuāng
及老庄。

jīng zǐ tōng
经子通，
dú zhū shǐ
读诸史。
kǎo shì xì
考世系，
zhī zhōng shǐ
知终始。

shǐ
史

zì xī nóng
自羲农，
zhì huáng dì
至黄帝。
hào sān huáng
号三皇，
jū shàng shì
居上世。

táng yǒu yú
唐有虞，
hào èr dì
号二帝。
xiāng yī xùn
相揖逊，
chēng shèng shì
称盛世。

xià yǒu yǔ
夏有禹，
shāng yǒu tāng
商有汤。
zhōu wén wǔ
周文武，
chēng sān wáng
称三王。

xià chuán zǐ
夏传子，
jiā tiān xià
家天下。
sì bǎi zài
四百载，
qiān xià shè
迁夏社。

tāng fá xià
汤伐夏，
guó hào shāng
国号商。
liù bǎi zài
六百载，
zhì zhòu wáng
至纣亡。

zhōu wǔ wáng
周武王，
shǐ zhū zhòu
始诛纣。
bā bǎi zài
八百载，
zuì cháng jiǔ
最长久。

zhōu zhé dōng
周辙东，
wáng gāng zhuì
王纲坠。
chěng gān gē
逞干戈，
shàng yóu shuō
尚游说。

shǐ chūn qiū
始春秋，
zhōng zhàn guó
终战国。
wǔ bà qiáng
五霸强，
qī xióng chū
七雄出。

yíng qín shì
嬴秦氏，
shǐ jiān bìng
始兼并。
chuán èr shì
传二世，
chǔ hàn zhēng
楚汉争。

gāo zǔ xīng
高祖兴，
hàn yè jiàn
汉业建。
zhì xiào píng
至孝平，
wáng mǎng cuàn
王莽篡。

guāng wǔ xīng
光武兴，
wéi dōng hàn
为东汉。
sì bǎi nián
四百年，
zhōng yú xiàn
终于献。

wèi shǔ wú
魏蜀吴，
zhēng hàn dǐng
争汉鼎。
hào sān guó
号三国，
qì liǎng jìn
迄两晋。

sòng qí jì
宋齐继，
liáng chén chéng
梁陈承。
wéi nán cháo
为南朝，
dū jīn líng
都金陵。

běi yuán wèi
北元魏，
fēn dōng xī
分东西。
yǔ wén zhōu
宇文周，
xīng gāo qí
兴高齐。

dài zhì suí
迨至隋，
yī tǔ yǔ
一土宇。
bù zài chuán
不再传，
shī tǒng xù
失统绪。

táng gāo zǔ
唐高祖，
qǐ yì shī
起义师。
chú suí luàn
除隋乱，
chuàng guó jī
创国基。

èr shí chuán
二十传，
sān bǎi zài
三百载。
liáng miè zhī
梁灭之，
guó nǎi gǎi
国乃改。

liáng táng jìn
梁唐晋，
jí hàn zhōu
及汉周。
chēng wǔ dài
称五代，
jiē yǒu yóu
皆有由。

yán sòng xīng
炎宋兴，
shòu zhōu chán
受周禅。
shí bā chuán
十八传，
nán běi hùn
南北混。

liáo yǔ jīn
辽与金，
jiē chēng dì
皆称帝。
yuán miè jīn
元灭金，
jué sòng shì
绝宋世。

yú tú guǎng
舆图广，
chāo qián dài
超前代。
jiǔ shí nián
九十年，
guó zuò fèi
国祚废。

tài zǔ xīng
太祖兴，
guó dà míng
国大明。
hào hóng wǔ
号洪武，
dū jīn líng
都金陵。

dài chéng zǔ
迨成祖，
qiān yān jīng
迁燕京。
shí liù shì
十六世，
zhì chóng zhēn
至崇祯。

yān huò hòu
阉祸后，
kòu nèi hòng
寇内讧。
chuǎng nì biàn
闯逆变，
shén qì zhōng
神器终。

gǔ jīn shǐ
古今史，
quán zài zī
全在兹。
zài zhì luàn
载治乱，
zhī xīng shuāi
知兴衰。

shǐ suī fán
史虽繁，
dú yǒu cì
读有次。
shǐ jì yī
史记一，
hàn shū èr
汉书二。

hòu hàn sān
后汉三，
guó zhì sì
国志四。
jiān zhèng jīng
兼证经，
cān tōng jiàn
参通鉴。

dú shǐ zhě
读史者，
kǎo shí lù
考实录。
tōng gǔ jīn
通古今，
ruò qīn mù
若亲目。

qín
勤

kǒu ér sòng
口而诵，
xīn ér wéi
心而惟。
zhāo yú sī
朝于斯，
xī yú sī
夕于斯。

xī zhòng ní
昔仲尼，
shī xiàng tuó
师项橐。
gǔ shèng xián
古圣贤，
shàng qín xué
尚勤学。

zhào zhōng lìng
赵中令，
dú lǔ lùn
读鲁论。
bǐ jì shì
彼既仕，
xué qiě qín
学且勤。

pī pú biān
披蒲编，
xiāo zhú jiǎn
削竹简。
bǐ wú shū
彼无书，
qiě zhī miǎn
且知勉。

tóu xuán liáng
头悬梁，
zhuī cì gǔ
锥刺股。
bǐ bù jiào
彼不教，
zì qín kǔ
自勤苦。

rú nāng yíng
如囊萤，
rú yìng xuě
如映雪。
jiā suī pín
家虽贫，
xué bù chuò
学不辍。

rú fù xīn
如负薪，
rú guà jiǎo
如挂角。
shēn suī láo
身虽劳，
yóu kǔ zhuó
犹苦卓。

sū lǎo quán
苏老泉，
èr shí qī
二十七。
shǐ fā fèn
始发愤，
dú shū jí
读书籍。

bǐ jì lǎo
彼既老，
yóu huǐ chí
犹悔迟。
ěr xiǎo shēng
尔小生，
yí zǎo sī
宜早思。

ruò liáng hào
若梁灏，
bā shí èr
八十二。
duì dà tíng
对大廷，
kuí duō shì
魁多士。

bǐ jì chéng
彼既成，
zhòng chēng yì
众称异。
ěr xiǎo shēng
尔小生，
yí lì zhì
宜立志。

yíng bā suì
莹八岁，
néng yǒng shī
能咏诗。
mì qī suì
泌七岁，
néng fù qí
能赋棋。

bǐ yǐng wù
彼颖悟，
rén chēng qí
人称奇。
ěr yòu xué
尔幼学，
dāng xiào zhī
当效之。

cài wén jī
蔡文姬，
néng biàn qín
能辨琴。
xiè dào yùn
谢道韫，
néng yǒng yín
能咏吟。

bǐ nǚ zǐ
彼女子，
qiě cōng mǐn
且聪敏。
ěr nán zǐ
尔男子，
dāng zì jǐng
当自警。

táng liú yàn
唐刘晏，
fāng qī suì
方七岁。
jǔ shén tóng
举神童，
zuò zhèng zì
作正字。

bǐ suī yòu
彼虽幼，
shēn yǐ shì
身已仕。
yǒu wéi zhě
有为者，
yì ruò shì
亦若是。

quǎn shǒu yè
犬守夜，
jī sī chén
鸡司晨。
gǒu bù xué
苟不学，
hé wéi rén
曷为人。

cán tǔ sī
蚕吐丝，
fēng niàng mì
蜂酿蜜。
rén bù xué
人不学，
bù rú wù
不如物。

yòu ér xué
幼而学，
zhuàng ér xíng
壮而行，
shàng zhì jūn
上致君，
xià zé mín
下泽民。

yáng míng shēng
扬名声，
xiǎn fù mǔ
显父母。
guāng yú qián
光于前，
yù yú hòu
裕于后。

rén yí zǐ
人遗子，
jīn mǎn yíng
金满籯。
wǒ jiào zǐ
我教子，
wéi yī jīng
唯一经。

qín yǒu gōng
勤有功，
xì wú yì
戏无益。
jiè zhī zāi
戒之哉，
yí miǎn lì
宜勉力。

About the Author

Zhao Yan-chun is Professor of English at Shanghai University and Guest Professor at Beijing Language and Culture University, Sun Yat-sen University, Beijing Agriculture University and some other universities, after his tenure as Special Professor of Tianjin, one of Tianjin's One Thousand Talents, director of the Center for Language, Literature and Culture at Tianjin Foreign Studies University while being Vice President of the Academic Committee at the same university. He is Director of the Research Center for Chinese Culture and Translation at Beijing Language and Culture University, Member of the Academic Committee of the International Society of East and West, Editor of *Translating China*, Editorial Board Member of *Guangyi* in Taiwan National Chengchi University, Vice President of China Language Education Association, Research Fellow of the International Association for East-West Studies, and Member of Academic Committee of Mericet, India. His academic interests include translation studies, linguistics and philosophy. He has written extensively about the relationship between philosophy, language, literature and translation and has published 7 monographs and 13 classic translations, and 5 text books in additon to a great number of academic papers. He adheres to the principle of translating poesie into poesie and classic into classic. His *Three Word Primer in English Rhyme* has been widely reported by national and local media such as *People's Daily*, *China Daily* and so on, acclaimed as the unprecedented Chinese-English translation, the best, the choice, the cream.

作者简介

赵彦春，上海大学教授、天津市特聘教授、天津外国语大学外国语言文学文化研究中心主任、天津外国语大学学术委员会副主任、北京语言大学中国文化翻译与传播研究中心主任、国际东西方学会学术委员会委员、国际学术期刊 *Translating China* 主编、台湾政治大学广译编委、中国语言教育研究会副会长、天津外文学会常务副会长、天津外语专业研究生创新论坛常务副主任、中山大学兼职教授、中国农业大学兼职教授、天津科技大学客座教授、天津财经大学客座教授、印度 Mericet 大学学术委员会委员。涉猎哲学、语言学、翻译学等多门专业，在哲学、语言、文学和翻译的关系上著述甚丰，除科研论文外，出版专著 7 部，译著 13 部，编审教材 5 部。翻译实践上坚守以诗译诗，以经译经的准则。英韵三字经是有史以来第一部以三个英语单词对应三个汉字的偶韵体三字经译文，被新华社、人民日报、光明日报、中国日报、二十一世纪英文报、渤海日报、今晚报、天津广播电台以及今日头条、网易等各大知名媒体广泛报道，被誉为『有史以来最美汉英翻译』『神翻译』『神还原』。

图书在版编目(CIP)数据

英韵《三字经》：插图本：汉英对照 / 赵彦春译注. --
北京：高等教育出版社，2017.9（2020.5 重印）
ISBN 978-7-04-048356-7
I. 1 英 … II. 1 赵 … III. 1 古汉语 – 启蒙读物 – 汉、英
IV. H194.1

中国版本图书馆 CIP 数据核字（2017）第 188323 号

英韵
三字经
（插图本）

YINGYUN
SANZIJING

Three Word Primer in English Rhyme

With Illustrations

策划编辑	徐莉萍　刘清田
责任编辑	洪世英
书籍设计	张志奇
插图	张申申
英文朗诵	［美］Jem Riche
中文朗诵	翟昕辰
责任校对	刘娟娟
责任印制	韩刚
出版发行	高等教育出版社
社址	北京市西城区德外大街 4 号
邮政编码	100120
印刷	北京雅昌艺术印刷有限公司
开本	787mm × 1092mm　1/16
印张	15.75
字数	200 千字
购书热线	010-58581118
咨询电话	400-810-0598
网址	http://www.hep.edu.cn
	http://www.hep.com.cn
网上订购	http://www.hepmall.com.cn
	http://www.hepmall.com
	http://www.hepmall.cn
版次	2017 年 9 月第 1 版
印次	2020 年 5 月第 2 次印刷
定价	139.00 元

ISBN 978-7-04-048356-7
9 787040 483567 >
定价 139.00 元